PRAISE FOR *CHANG*

"A must-have survival kit for leaders in all industries."

—**SAM WOODS,** VP of Business Development,
JORI International

"After reading *Change the Sandler Way,* I came away with a clear understanding of how to apply Sandler principles to support organizational change. This is one book that will become a personal reference tool for me in my career."

—**REBECCA WOOD,** Director of Member Services,
Calgary Chamber of Commerce

"This is a book about leveraging the communication side of change management. While it may be first understood as a sales-related book, it is much more at the essence of exceptional sales—effective communications among people."

—**ROB SCHMIDT,** President of reBox Creative Inc.

"An excellent roadmap to help managers and business owners navigate smoothly through organizational change."

—**KRISTA HERMANSON,** CEO, Krista Hermanson Design

"A must-read for leaders who are implementing growth and change in their organizations and for employees who strive to excel."

—**MELISSA ZOLLER,** Owner, MHZ Consulting

MORE PRAISE FOR *CHANGE THE SANDLER WAY*

"Change is inevitable in any organization, and how the transition is handled can either end up in success or failure. Hamish outlines effective tools, approaches and insights to equip and challenge leaders at every level to lead their teams to success."

—**KIM SMITH,** Community Manager,
Capital Ideas/Postmedia Network

"Offers great insights into affecting change in an organization. I highly recommend reading this book before undertaking your next change initiative."

—**JEFF BORSCHOWA,** Growth Strategist,
Business Evolution Consulting Inc.

"I don't think I will try to make a big change in my company again without reviewing this book."

—**WENDY COOMBS,** Director/CEO,
Momentum Health

CHANGE
THE SANDLER WAY

Understanding the Human Dynamics
That Cause New Initiatives to Succeed

HAMISH KNOX

Sandler Training

Paperback ISBN: 978-0-692-75081-0
E-book: ISBN: 978-0-692-75082-7

Printed and bound in the UK by 4edge Limited

To my wife Kim; my daughters Taylor and Lexi;
my coach John Shrum; my mentor Robert Schmidt;
my team Nisha and Ashley; and Kru Sandra Bastian,
who prompted the greatest transitions in my life.

CONTENTS

FOREWORD

Nelson Mandela once said, "May your choices reflect your hopes, not your fears." It's a powerful, memorable distinction—one that can benefit any manager who faces the daunting task of getting a team to adapt to a new strategic plan, a new system, or a new market environment.

Helping people to expand their comfort zones, supporting them as they adapt to unfamiliar situations, challenging them to embrace new opportunities—all of these are, in the final analysis, variations on one of a leader's most important responsibilities: modeling and reinforcing the essential habit of choosing aspiration over fear. This book is an invaluable asset for managers who are looking for the best ways to do that.

Hamish Knox has written a comprehensive, detailed playbook in support of constructive personal responses to organizational change. The heart of his book is the selling system devised by our company's founder, David Sandler, who believed salespeople should never have to sacrifice their personal integrity in the delivery of win/win outcomes to themselves and their customers. Now Hamish demonstrates just how well those same core Sandler® principles apply to leaders who strive to secure win/win outcomes for themselves and their team members.

We live in a world where rapid, often unpredictable change sometimes seems to be the only constant in the workplace. That can be a scary reality. *Change the Sandler Way* is essential reading for those who are ready, willing, and eager to move beyond fear and remake their world for the better.

Shaun and Anneli Thomson
Sandler Training

INTRODUCTION

Technically, this book is not about change. It's a book about transitions.

A book on change would be no longer than a pamphlet because change is external and impersonal. For example, a company changes by switching from one vendor to another or by starting an employee benefits program. Change is an on/off switch.

Transitions, on the other hand, are internal and personal to each individual who is affected by a change either directly or indirectly. This book is about the four stages of transitions that you and each member of your team will experience, from the moment you start thinking about making a change, through the "end" of that change, to the next change ahead—whether it's change you create (e.g., implementing CRM) or change that is forced on you externally (e.g., new salient government regulations).

There are four stages of transition that many people experience when making a successful adjustment to a new work situation, and eight common, potentially negative consequences that are likely to accompany any organizational change initiative. Leaders who understand these four stages and who understand the human dynamics behind the eight most common challenges can improve their odds of success.

This book is for such leaders. It explores how beliefs, judgments, and actions related to transitions create results. Beliefs, judgments, and actions form a "belief wheel" based on an outlook of limitation or of possibility that ultimately determines whether the change and transition will be successful. You'll learn more about the belief wheel in Chapter 1.

How you communicate before, during, and after transition and how your team interprets your communication goes a long way to making any new initiative either smooth or bumpy. Also, the life scripts that are hardwired into your brain from childhood can affect how you yourself transition, without your being conscious of how those scripts are guiding you. It's like that for everyone. We all have scripts.

Those scripts will create the angels, agnostics, and atheists of your new initiative. Any script can be detrimental to successfully implementing change and transition in your organization.

The ultimate success or failure of a new initiative and the transitions of each team member rest with their leader. Proper implementation of a new initiative, including planning, will help you to manage your team's transitions better since you will be prepared to handle the common challenges that may arise.

For you to successfully lead your business, you must remember the forgotten side of new initiatives—your people—and become comfortable with supporting them as individuals through their transitions. This requires no small degree of honest self-assessment on your part. Therefore, many of the exercises you will find in this book ask questions that might seem quite personal. Answer as best as you can to gain deeper value from this book.

WHO OR WHAT IS SANDLER?

Sandler Systems, Inc. is the world's largest leadership, management, sales, and customer care development company.

Sandler trainers enable clients to be successful by design instead of by default through tools developed by David Sandler, the founder of Sandler Training and the creator of the Sandler Selling System® methodology.

Throughout this book are references to Sandler Rules, which are short phrases that David Sandler would use to illustrate a concept or describe how human beings interact with each other.

If you are curious to learn more about Sandler Training, visit www.sandler.com.

CHAPTER 1

So You're Going to Change the Company?

Business people no longer have the luxury of avoiding organizational change internally and externally. They can, however, train themselves to recognize leading indicators and prepare their teams to benefit from the change—or at the very least mitigate any negative impacts. A great tool that supports a deeper understanding of this process is known as the belief wheel.

THE BELIEF WHEEL

It is people's outlook, beliefs, judgments, and (in)actions that allow them to benefit, mitigate, or be left behind by changes in and out of their control. The belief wheel shows how this takes place.

BELIEFS

RESULTS   JUDGMENTS

ACTIONS

CASE IN POINT: PRESIDENT SABOTAGES OWN CHANGE EFFORT

To avoid being swallowed up by a larger company, the president of an engineering firm wanted to grow his business beyond the small, highly specialized organization that it had become. He brought on a senior technical expert and a salesperson, promising both equity in the expanded venture, and set about creating processes and procedures for a larger firm. While the president had a compelling vision, the truth was he believed himself to be a contractor. This belief caused him to judge that he had to do all the work himself, taking on the action of doing work that others had been hired to do. As a result, the president alienated his tech expert and salesperson. Morale and productivity plummeted. Within the year, the technical person had been let go, the salesperson had quit, and the president had effectively shut down the firm and settled back into his "consultant" comfort zone.

CREATING A SELF-FULFILLING PROPHECY

A person's outlook develops from childhood and carries forward into adulthood built on the media and associates he chooses. His outlook can also be rooted in the degree of control he feels he has over his life.

If you believe you have little control over your life, whether that's because you grew up in an oppressive society or because you choose to believe negative news or people, your outlook tends to be one of limitation.

If you believe you have a lot of control over your life, your outlook tends to be one of possibility. However, having an outlook of possibility doesn't mean that your change will always be successful.

Your outlook acts as a filter that accepts information that is consistent with your outlook and rejects information that is inconsistent. As you continue to filter out information that is inconsistent with your outlook, you will form beliefs. If you have an outlook of limitation (e.g., "change is hard"), you will develop a belief consistent with that outlook (e.g., "change will take a lot of time and effort").

Beliefs aren't rational creations. They typically result from an emotional reaction to an external stimulus, which is why the judgments resulting from beliefs often come out as absolutes (e.g., "around here, change is always a waste of time.")

Judgments cause people to act or not act. For example, people who judge change to "always" be a waste of time are unlikely to explore how it might benefit them or their organization.

The (in)actions people take then reinforce their outlook, which strengthens their beliefs, which initiates their judgments, which causes further (in)action. Once set in motion, this self-fulfilling prophecy leads to nowhere.

Exercise: Your Self-Fulfilling Prophecy

Think of a change you implemented, personally or professionally, in the last nine months, preferably one that wasn't as successful as you hoped.

_____

_____

_____

_____

Appreciating that hindsight tends to cause you to remember something as being better or worse than it actually was, rate, on a scale of 1–10, how you felt about the potential success of your change prior to implementing. In this case, 1 means "destined to fail" and 10 means "sure to succeed."

Estimation of potential success

1   2   3   4   5   6   7   8   9   10

Next, write down the beliefs you had about that change after it wasn't as successful as you hoped (e.g., "I can't believe that didn't work," or "There's no reason to try that again").

_____

_____

_____

_____

Now write down the judgments you made about that change after it didn't succeed (e.g., "I'm the wrong person for this," [internal] or "They wouldn't listen to me" [external]). Notice whether the excuse is internal or external.

_____

_____

_____

_____

Finally, write down the actions you took or didn't take after you abandoned your change (e.g., do a post-mortem).

_____

_____

_____

_____

Exercise: Creating a New Prophecy

Adjusting your outlook to one of possibility, especially after a failed change effort, won't happen without reframing your beliefs and judgments and selecting new actions.

Reframe the beliefs you wrote down in the last exercise to come from an outlook of possibility (e.g., "I can't believe that didn't work," becomes, "What can I learn from this?").

_____

_____

_____

_____

Next do the same for the judgments you wrote down previously (e.g., "I'm the wrong person for this," becomes, "I can't do it alone").

———————————————————————————

———————————————————————————

———————————————————————————

———————————————————————————

Finally, write down the actions you could take to re-implement the change (e.g., analyzing previous plan, re-adjusting, finding others to help implement and manage).

———————————————————————————

———————————————————————————

———————————————————————————

———————————————————————————

CHANGE VS. TRANSITION

As a leader you must always keep in mind that when you talk about change, you're actually talking about two separate events: change for your organization (whether that organization is a corporation or a family) and transition for the people who make up the organization.

Put another way, change is external and impersonal (e.g., a government changing an income tax rate), whereas a transition is internal and personal (e.g., a citizen transitioning to having more or less discretionary income based on the new income tax rate).

Change and transition are symbiotic. Change can't happen without transition and transition can't happen without change. However, transitions must be essentially complete for a change to be considered a success. Without the people in an organization transitioning to a new way of behavior, change won't happen.

CASE IN POINT: FACTORY GETS NEW BONUS STRUCTURE

The management of a manufacturing company wanted to develop a new bonus structure for employees on the shop floor. The current bonus structure was paid annually, with each employee's share based mostly on seniority. The proposed bonus structure would be paid quarterly based on successfully increasing safety by reducing problems such as days lost to injury.

This company already had an exemplary safety record, so their employees didn't need to transition to a focus on creating a safer work environment. Their transition rather was accepting that they would now have control over their variable compensation when previously the only control they had was adding another year of seniority.

After a series of meetings with all shop-floor employees during which company executives encouraged questions and discussion, the majority of employees accepted the new bonus structure. Those who didn't left prior to the first quarterly bonuses being paid out.

All humans go through four stages of transition. The length of time people spend in each stage depends on their preferred communication style and their hardwired scripts, which this book will address in separate chapters.

THE FOUR STAGES OF TRANSITION

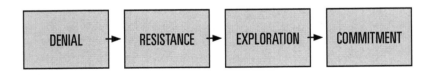

Denial

The strength of an individual's denial that change is happening relates directly to how sudden and personal that individual feels it is.

A clear illustration of denial would be after a death in an individual's family, especially if that individual was close to the deceased. For instance, if you hear from an authoritative source that your dear aunt has passed away in an automobile accident, and your initial response is, "That's impossible, I just saw her yesterday," that's an example of denial.

Salespeople typically remain in denial about adjustments to their compensation plans, even when it affects their personal income if they are unable to draw a clear line between the new plan and an increase in income.

Denial is also strong in individuals who experience repeated change without any clear conclusions. For example, a child who moves to a new town or school or an employee who gets a new manager every year or two will have a strong denial response to a new situation.

Many leaders I've worked with find the denial stage in their employees frustrating because they themselves have already worked their way through the four stages of transition. But, as David Sandler said, "It's never about you." Denying the denial stage will impede your change effort by causing frustration for both you and your employees. Many leaders make the mistake of assuming that a new communication plan and a couple of meetings will address any issue. They usually end up focusing only on externals.

When individuals are in the denial phase of transition, they may say things like, "That won't affect me," "This too shall pass," "I wish they'd finish one thing before moving to another," "This isn't happening," or "I hear lots of talk, but I don't see much action."

While it may be difficult for you as a leader to hear those statements from your employees, especially if they come from core members of your team, recognize that the employees are starting on the path to transitioning and encourage them to explore their denial with questions.

If they say one of the above comments, counter with a question that helps them articulate what they're feeling. For instance:

- "That won't affect me." "What makes you say it won't affect you?"
- "This too shall pass." "What do you mean?"
- "I wish they'd finish one thing before moving to another." "Would you give me an example?"
- "This isn't happening." "What makes you say that?"
- "I hear lots of talk, but I don't see much action." "Tell me more about that."

The last suggestion is an example of an "unasked" question, which prompts someone to talk even though you didn't directly ask a question. (By the way, you'll find much more guidance on framing effective questions in the Appendix of this book.)

Resistance

Resistance typically creates the most conflict during a change. While you might be able to cajole or badger people through denial, when they hit resistance they will dig in hard.

A wise leader will encourage the free expression of resistance because it means that the team is moving forward in their transition instead of staying stuck in the status quo.

As with denial, resistance can be frustrating for a leader who already went through that stage, especially because it can make employees sound like they are directly challenging their leader.

Statements like, "That will never work," "If that happens, I'm out of here," "Which idiot thought of that?" or "Are you crazy?" indicate that someone is going through the resistance stage of transition.

The cliché, "It's the quiet ones you have to watch," fits well with employees in the resistance stage. The quiet ones will resist your change covertly, either through passive noncompliance or indirect sabotage, by turning their colleagues against it. Covert resistance is strongest when leaders punish overt resistance or when change is happening in a low-trust, hierarchical organization that discourages open dialogue.

To reduce covert resistance and successfully navigate your team's resistance stage as a leader, remember this classic piece of advice: "Be emotionally unattached from the outcome." Remaining emotionally unattached may be extremely challenging when you created the proposed change or are championing it to your team, but it is essential.

CASE IN POINT: LEADER ALLOWING
EXPLORATION OF DENIAL AND RESISTANCE

Leslie's direct report Tabitha stormed into Leslie's office after a company-wide memo went out announcing changes to the organization's employee retirement savings plan.

TABITHA (brandishing a print-out of the memo): Leslie, what's this about changing the retirement savings plan?

LESLIE: Thanks for asking, Tabitha. What's your concern?

TABITHA: This can't be happening now! I plan to retire in eight years, and I built all of my savings goals on our current plan.

LESLIE: I appreciate you sharing that with me, Tabitha. What's your concern?

TABITHA: I feel like long-term employees are being punished.

LESLIE: Hmm, what makes you say that?

TABITHA: Because they're taking away accelerators for years of service.

LESLIE: Oh. Where is that in the announcement?

TABITHA: It says it right...Oh. I guess when I read, "modifying accelerators," I took that to mean that the years of service accelerator was going away.

LESLIE: That's totally understandable. Just a quick question—what would happen if we put that assumption on hold for a couple of minutes so we could talk it through and then see if it's accurate?

TABITHA: That would be great!

By allowing Tabitha to explore her feelings of denial and resistance through specific questions that didn't address Tabitha's emotional statements, Leslie managed to move Tabitha quickly to the third stage of transition: exploration.

Exploration

Once employees are through resistance, they begin to explore the benefits of the change and how they can take it from proposal to implementation and management.

Ideally, what employees discover through exploration is that when a change benefits their organization, it can also benefit them personally. Leaders who know each team member's personal goals can make the exploration stage of transition easier by coaching them through discovering how they can now reach their goals faster or easier.

CASE IN POINT: ONE DAY OFF DOESN'T MEAN ALL AT ONCE

Aidan's direct report Joe is exploring how a department recommendation of working longer hours Monday through Thursday to get every Friday off would affect him since his spouse also works and they have a child in elementary school.

JOE: Aidan, thanks for setting aside this time for me.

AIDAN: Sure, Joe. What did you want to discuss?

JOE: Well, I'm struggling to figure out how I make the new hours work on the home front. Since both my spouse and I work, I'm anxious that our son will spend a lot of time in after-school care instead of with us.

AIDAN: That makes sense. How can I support you?

JOE: Is there any way that I can avoid the extra hours? My colleagues are all excited about the new schedule, but a lot of them are single, and none of them have kids, so they're totally comfortable working longer.

AIDAN: Fair question, Joe. If I remember, one of your goals this year was to pick up your son from school every day.

JOE: That's right. I planned to talk to you about it, and then that memo came out on our first day back from the holiday break.

AIDAN: What would you have shared with me if we had had that discussion?

JOE: I thought I could come in early each day. I'd still owe you some time, and I couldn't come in more than 30 minutes early. Let's say I come in early, work through lunch and work Fridays. That way I could get my son from school each day and still keep my commitments to you and my colleagues.

AIDAN: I appreciate your plan, Joe, but I feel working through lunch every day would end up hurting your productivity because we all need breaks. Come in early, take a 30-minute break for lunch, and work Fridays. How's that sound to you? You could still leave early on Friday to get your son from school.

JOE: I really appreciate your being flexible, Aidan.

Aidan has given Joe a leader's three greatest gifts—permission, protection, and potency.

- **Permission:** Often a team member's biggest fear, especially during change, is failing. Leaders should give permission to fail (because people will) to reduce resistance and encourage exploration.

- **Protection:** When a team member fails, don't use it as a "gotcha" moment. Instead, turn that opportunity into a coaching moment and support your team member to move to the exploration and commitment phase of his transition.

- **Potency:** Allow your team members to perform in their new roles without you micromanaging or doing things for them. In cases where a failure could be catastrophic (like flying an airplane), potency could include practice in a simulator. In a case where failure could result in reduced productivity or lost sales opportunities, potency may include role-play and support documentation.

When you are a leader letting team members explore their own path to the top of the mountain that you defined (the change), it can be frustrating because you might believe that you've already figured out the best way to get there. While letting your team explore different routes to your mountaintop will increase your chances of a successful change, you'll also want to define a time limit for exploration and any out-of-bounds areas. Otherwise, you're likely to have at least one team member become attached to a path that would require additional time, money, and resources that you may be unwilling or unable to invest.

Commitment

The final stage of transition is an individual's commitment to new behavior facilitating successful adaptation to the new situation. Commitment is the point at which people become personally accountable for taking the actions necessary to integrate themselves into an environment that was once unfamiliar to them.

The key concept here is personal responsibility. The great Russian novelist Leo Tolstoy once noted that people love to talk about change, but aren't always willing to change themselves. People who have reached the fourth stage, the stage of commitment, are willing to change themselves. Leaders can leverage committed employees to champion change to others who are at earlier stages of transition. Employees at the commitment stage can relate peer-to-peer to their colleagues at earlier stages.

MANAGING TRANSITION

For your change to be successful, you must be comfortable managing your employees' transition. Leaders who haven't given permission, protection, and potency to their team members typically push back on the team's denial and resist any resistance. A leader who does one or both works against the successful implementation of the change.

Just as the transition process has four parts, managing transition in your team has four steps.

1) RECOGNIZE AND PREDICT THE DYNAMICS OF TRANSITIONING

Successful change requires managing the leading indicators of transition in your team members.

Leading indicators of transition are what people say or do or what they don't say or do when facing a change. For example, what if one of your team members, who regularly invites others out for coffee or lunch, starts eating lunch alone in his office or going out alone? This unusual behavior indicates that the team member may be in denial about the change. Noticing this is an opportunity for you as team leader to support him in working through his transition.

As leaders, understanding how teams transition will help you recognize these stages in your team members.

Exercise: How You Transition

Think of a change you went through in the past 12 months, personally or professionally, preferably one that wasn't conceived of by you. As you reflect back, make note of what you did or didn't say or do in each phase of transition. How did you experience the four stages?

Denial

_____

_____

_____

_____

Resistance

_____

_____

_____

_____

Exploration

_____

_____

_____

_____

Commitment

_____

_____

_____

_____

It's likely you will develop a sense of what is going to happen in the discussion with employees based on your observation of an individual's actions, words, or body language. Like a poker player learning the "tells" of the other players at the table, as you observe individuals around you going through the transition you will learn to identify their current stage and what they are likely to say or do next.

As you gain this kind of expertise, resist any urge to directly predict what they will say or do next. Doing so would be a quick way to break rapport—your team members will feel like you are parenting them. While the transition process is predictable, completing each stage of the process isn't a guarantee for each team member. Because you lead humans instead of robots, you might have a strong sense of what others will say or do next based on your experience and their recent behavior. But until an individual actualy says or does something, you don't know for sure.

David Sandler gave a powerful tool to use when one might feel compelled to predict what another will say or do next: "I get the sense that... Is that fair to say?" Stating your expectations in that way gives the other person an opportunity to either accept or deny your statement.

CASE IN POINT: I GET THE SENSE THAT...

Darla's direct report Micha is in the denial phase of transition. Darla needs to move Micha quickly through resistance and into exploration because she needs him to champion the change to his peers. This scene begins mid-conversation.

MICHA: Darla, I can't believe our commission plan is changing.

DARLA: Why's that, Micha?

MICHA: Because our commission plan changes every year! We hear lots from you about "consistency" and "predictability," but it's hard to stay consistent and predict my income year-to-year if we get a new plan every 12 months.

DARLA: Micha, my sense is the new compensation plan isn't the real issue. Is that fair to say?

MICHA: I guess so. We're frustrated that the payout on one of our core products was reduced significantly, and we're not sure how to even get back to where we were commission-wise last year.

DARLA: Thanks for helping me understand, Micha. If we worked through that together, would you be comfortable sharing our results with your colleagues?

MICHA: Sure, if you can show me how to at least get back to where I was last year.

Micha only had two possible responses to Darla's "fair" question: "No," to which Darla would have replied, "What would be fair?" or "Yes," which Darla helped him then explore.

2) STRATEGICALLY PLAN WAYS TO REDUCE RESISTANCE

Resistance will happen during change. Discounting resistance in yourself and your team will impede both current and future change efforts.

"Discounting" is a psychological term that means minimizing another's statement. If you have children, or if your remember from your own childhood, you may have said or heard in response to "There's a monster under my bed": "Honey, there's no monster. Go back to bed." "There's no monster" is discounting that child's statement of fear.

Discounting might sound like, "Don't worry about it," in response to an employee saying, "How will this affect me?" By discounting the employee's fear-based question, the leader promotes covert resistance to the change because the employee now believes that the leader isn't honest about its effects.

In certain situations, such as layoffs or mergers, there are legal reasons why a leader can't be completely open with employees. In those cases, it's better for leaders to share with their team how much they are allowed to discuss instead of what they are allowed to discuss. Leaders who dive into the *what* will end up in a box of their own making. Humans aren't wired to stop asking questions when someone says, "I can't tell you any more than I have."

Exercise: Resistance Planning and Elimination

Write down a change that you plan to implement that will affect more than just you in the next nine months.

_____

_____

_____

_____

Based on the people on your team, what can you reasonably expect them to say or do to resist this change overtly or covertly (e.g., threaten to quit, "forget" to use the new system, post an anonymous blog, etc.)?

_____

_____

_____

_____

What could you do as leader to proactively eliminate or reduce the impact of those resistance behaviors in your team (e.g., individual coaching, team meetings, email updates, etc.)?

_____

_____

_____

_____

3) EXPAND YOUR LEADERSHIP COMFORT ZONE TO MANAGE CHANGE

Working with your employees through their transition will mean you as their leader will need to be comfortable having direct, open, difficult conversations. A belief on your part that "they'll come around eventually" will cause you more pain than the awkwardness you might feel having a conversation with a team member who is in denial or resistance.

The hardest four inches to travel is from one's brain to one's mouth. Even if you feel comfortable having a difficult conversation with a team member, your conversations will be more positive and create more real action if you practice. Put another way, remember to role-play. Yes, role-play your difficult conversations with a coach, mentor, or fellow executive who has the same "clearance" to discuss the change as you.

When preparing for a difficult conversation, you're likely to put pressure on yourself to "get it right." When people start thinking this way, it usually means they have created an ideal outcome in their brain to which they have become emotionally attached. However, this will keep you stuck in your comfort zone. You're unlikely to reach your ideal outcome in your first few conversations, which will cause you to get discouraged and to fall back into former patterns. When any activity, such as a difficult conversation, makes you uncomfortable, even doing the activity poorly at first is the win.

Another part of expanding your comfort zone to support your employees through transition is to empathize with them. Strip everything away, and you're just two humans having a conversation. Keeping legalities in mind, it's OK to say to an employee, "This is probably difficult for you. It would be difficult for me, too, if I were in your position." Being human with your team runs counter to much of traditional management and leadership training, but, especially when you are working with Millennials and the generations that follow them, employees want to know that their leader is a person, too.

A WORD ON MILLENNIALS

For the sake of this book, let's define "Millennial" as those born between 1980 and the early 2000s. Much research, including that by the Pew Research Center, has uncovered several characteristics of this group that apply to the successful implementation of change initiatives.

First, Millennials are used to collaborating and having their voices heard. As their leader, give them opportunities to help create the plan to implement and manage your new initiative.

Second, Millennials experienced several major world events during their formative years, such as the dot-com bubble, 9/11, and the global financial crisis in 2008. These events have created a need to seek trust and support from the individuals in their lives, including their leaders. When you lead Millennials through transitions, they must trust that you will support them. You can demonstrate this by your behavior, such as giving them an opportunity to express their feelings, rather than just saying they can trust you.

Third, because Millennials were exposed to the fragility of life and the instability of a "career" while they were still forming their worldview, they tend to be motivated by more than material bonuses or task completion. As the leader of Millennials going through a transition, give them the *why* behind the change and support them in finding their motivation to participate in its successful implementation.

As would be true with any demographic group, the notes above are just broad trends. Each Millennial on your team, like every other member of your team, is unique, with individual hopes, dreams, and fears. Using the above as "rules" for working with Millennials may instead damage your relationships. The best way to understand how to support each member of your team, no matter the demographic designation, is to treat each as an individual and ask questions instead of making assumptions based on broad-spectrum sociological research.

4) ANALYZE AND PLAN FOR CHANGE

We'll go deeper into planning for change in a later chapter, but what's critical to address here is that analysis and planning will give you and your team a sense of control. A core reason that people avoid change is that it means giving up control.

When some individuals feel out of control, they attempt to control everything, including people, data, or organizations beyond their reach (colleagues, the price of oil, government, etc.). Clearly, that is a useless effort. When you notice team members attempting to control beyond their reach, steer them back to what they can control.

Giving up keeps you rooted in the status quo, which is a pit stop on the way to irrelevance and death. Employees who appear to have given up are likely stuck in denial, so (gently) push them into resistance, exploration, and commitment, or suggest that they move on.

By letting go, you take the mental and emotional energy that would have been wasted and refocus it into achieving mastery of your change.

Just as there's no guarantee that you or all of your team members will complete the transition process, following the four steps outlined for managing transition doesn't mean that you will successfully manage the transition for all of your employees. Turnover is part of change. Part of your plan must include a strategy for replacing employees who move on by choice or by design.

THIS CHAPTER IN 45 SECONDS

- Leaders no longer have the luxury of avoiding change.
- Leaders can have an outlook of limitation or an outlook of possibility.
- Your outlook develops in childhood and is reinforced as you grow into adulthood from the media and associates you choose.
- The measure of control you feel over your life plays a large role in your outlook. Less control equals limitation; more control equals possibility.
- Your outlook acts as a filter for information that creates your beliefs.
- Beliefs aren't rational creations. This is why the judgments based on beliefs tend to be stated in absolutes (always, never).
- Judgments cause people to act or not act, which reinforces their outlook.
- Without reframing your beliefs, judgments, and actions from limitation to possibility, you create a self-fulfilling prophecy to nowhere.
- Change is external and impersonal; transition is internal and personal.
- For an organization to change, the members of that organization must first transition.
- Individuals transition through denial, resistance, exploration, and commitment.

- There's no guarantee that an individual will complete the transition process.
- To support your team through transition, you must first understand how you transition.
- The three most powerful gifts you can give your team are permission, protection, and potency.
- Practice observing how people in your life go through a transition. You will learn to predict what stage people are in and how they are likely to behave next.
- Using "I get the sense that..." gives team members permission to explore their feelings of denial and resistance.
- Encourage overt resistance to help your team move to exploration and commitment.
- Sandler Rule: Never manage anything you can't control.

CHAPTER 2

DISCussing Change

Open, effective communication is critical to successfully implementing and managing change. It's often mishandled by well-meaning executives who believe they are communicating openly and effectively, but who are really only communicating with the members of their team who share their communication style.

CASE IN POINT: TALKING TO YOURSELF

Mel, the president of a 112-person manufacturing company, was excited to announce the employee share buy-in plan he had spent the prior six months researching, crafting, tweaking, and re-tweaking.

He had a 15-slide PowerPoint deck prepared to his exact specifications, a comprehensive booklet, and an intranet page that explained his rationale for creating this plan. He also had the specific steps the president and his employees would go through to implement, extensive checklists for each step, and detailed formulas for how each category of employee (broken down by role and seniority) could earn the right to buy shares in the business.

Mel arranged an all-hands meeting for a Monday at 9:00 A.M. and started his presentation by reviewing the company's long history, which started with his father, and citing statistics on employee engagement and productivity from organizations that both had and did not have employee share buy-in programs. He then went through each of his PowerPoint slides, rushing at the end because he had already gone over the allotted time for this meeting by 15 minutes. He closed with, "Fill in your enrollment form before you leave Friday and send to our HR Manager."

The following Monday, the president was dismayed to learn that only 23 of the 112 employees had turned in their enrollment forms. At his management meeting that afternoon, five of his six managers shared that their teams were completely confused by the purpose of the program or felt the formula for earning the right to buy shares was too complicated.

Sandler has been a long-term fan of the DISC model of communication. This model shows how people like to give and receive information from both their hardwiring and how they adjust their communication style at work.

Note: If you consider yourself a DISC expert, and are familiar with its four distinct communication styles (Dominant, Influencer, Steady Relator, and Compliant), you may want to skip the next section and restart your reading at the sub-heading, "Your Team's DISC Style."

WHAT IS DISC?

DISC is a four-quadrant communications model based on the work of the psychologist William Moulton Marston.

Below is an example of the model, referred to as the "DISC Cross." Individuals on the Y-axis of the DISC cross are either "task oriented" communicators (top) or "people oriented" communicators (bottom). Individuals on the X-axis are either "active" communicators (right side) or "reserved" communicators (left side).

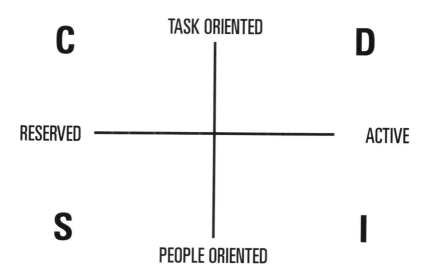

YOUR DISC STYLE

With DISC, there are no good or bad styles; there are simply communication activities that burn more or fewer mental calories for each style. For example, I am D-style, which means activities like making quick decisions and speaking directly burn few mental calories for me. On the flip side, I can do S-style activities that come naturally to the Steady Relator like nurturing and leadership by consensus, but those activities burn a lot of mental calories, so I can only do them for a short time.

Exercise: Your DISC Style

Read the four descriptions below and fill in the blanks, associating each of the four profiles with people you know. Then, pick the one that is most like you.

- Profile #1: "I'm a self-starter and a born risk-taker. I love solving problems. People say I have a healthy ego. I am direct in my dealings with you. I live to make decisions. I worry that someone will take advantage of me." A colleague who fits this description is _____.
  A friend or family member who fits this description is

  _____.

- Profile #2: "I'm extremely enthusiastic, talkative and persuasive. I draw energy from groups and thrive in social situations. I motivate others to achieve at a high level. I am usually optimistic. People sometimes say I'm too emotional. At my best, I'm downright inspirational. I worry about rejection." A colleague who fits this description is _____.

A friend or family member who fits this description is

_____.

- Profile #3: "I'm a great listener, loyal to the end, and eager to understand you. Some people call me the ultimate team player. Relationships mean a lot to me, and I don't like to let an ally down. I'm a peacekeeper. I'm reliable and dependable. I worry about a loss of security." A colleague who fits this description is _____. A friend or family member who fits this description is

  _____.

- Profile #4: "I have high standards. I work systematically. I'm precise. I find out the facts. I'm cautious, careful and conscientious. I'm rigorously analytical. It's extremely important to me to be accurate and well-organized. I worry about being forced to choose between quality and relationships because I will lean toward quality." A colleague who fits this description is _____. A friend or family member who fits this description is

  _____.

The profile that most closely describes me is

_____

- People you aligned with Behavioral Profile #1 are likely Dominants.
- People you aligned with Behavioral Profile #2 are likely Influencers.

- People you aligned with Behavioral Profile #3 are likely Steady Relators.
- People you aligned with Behavioral Profile #4 are likely Compliants.

Put it all together, and it spells DISC.

Most individuals are comfortable communicating in at least two if not three of the four DISC styles, so they will prefer one style but also use others. In very rare cases, individuals may be completely dominant in one style, which can make it very difficult for them to communicate effectively with others. There are plenty of examples of people who are strongly dominant in a given style adapting successfully, however. There are powerful incentives for such adaptations. As the martial arts adage goes, "What doesn't bend, breaks."

Let's look at each of these four groups in more depth.

D-STYLE CHARACTERISTICS (DOMINANTS)

Being task-oriented and active, D-style individuals are most comfortable communicating results, whether those are results of a decision or just that they made a decision. D-styles also burn fewer mental calories when directing conversations, setting goals, speaking directly (bluntly), and making decisions quickly.

D-styles burn a lot of mental calories when they feel forced to slow down and explain their decisions step-by-step. As they aren't people-oriented, under stress they tend to focus on task completion instead of supporting themselves or members of their team, which may prompt them to become rigid, top-down communicators.

A D-style's biggest fear is losing control. When D-styles sense they are losing control, they may seek to reassert their dominance over that situation, which can lead to poor decision making and damaged relationships.

I-STYLE CHARACTERISTICS (INFLUENCERS)

Being people-oriented and active, I-style individuals are most comfortable communicating with and about people, especially if their communication will generate excitement or happiness in their audience. I-styles burn fewer mental calories when discussing activities that involve lots of people interaction and creating multiple visions for their future or the future of their organization.

I-styles burn a lot of mental calories when they feel forced to dive into details or focus on one project exclusively. As they aren't task-oriented under stress, I-styles will seek to surround themselves with people who will give them reassurance.

An I-style's biggest fear is rejection. When I-styles sense they are about to say or do something that might cause rejection by others (friends, family, co-workers, employees, the online community), they will pull back and adjust their actions to what they feel will enhance or at least maintain their current approval level.

S-STYLE CHARACTERISTICS (STEADY RELATORS)

Being people-oriented and reserved, S-style individuals are most comfortable communicating with people they already know well, especially if that communication revolves around supporting each other. S-styles burn fewer mental calories when they seek consensus and ways to maintain stability in their team.

S-styles burn a lot of mental calories when they feel forced to make quick decisions, especially when those decisions don't account for the feelings of their team members. Under stress, S-styles will tend to withdraw into themselves and will fight to maintain the status quo.

An S-style's biggest fear is sudden change. S-styles may get behind it, but if the change is implemented too quickly for them, fails to account for the feelings of their team members, or is forced on them, they may shut down.

C-STYLE CHARACTERISTICS (COMPLIANTS)

Being task-oriented and reserved, C-style individuals are most comfortable discussing facts, figures, and process. C-styles burn fewer mental calories following established procedures and working with data.

C-styles burn a ton of mental calories when communication turns emotional or when they are required to interact with others in a non-formal setting, such as a networking event. Under stress, C-styles tend to fall into "paralysis of analysis" mode as they seek to gather an infinite amount of data before acting.

A C-style's biggest fear is being wrong. C-style individuals are unlikely to buy into change without getting all of their questions answered to their satisfaction.

YOUR TEAM'S DISC STYLE

Now think of your team, specifically your direct reports. Take a minute on the next page and place your team members (our clients typically use first and last initials) in the quadrant you feel best reflects each person's typical communication style.

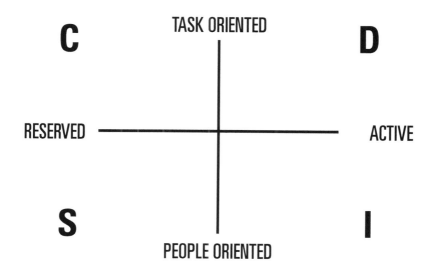

OVERWEIGHTED AND UNDERWEIGHTED TEAMS

Looking at where you placed your team members, you may notice that your team is overweighted to one quadrant or side of the DISC cross and underweighted in other areas. This is a natural occurrence in many organizations because humans tend to like to spend time with and hire people who communicate as they do. When my colleagues and I consult with clients on their recruiting process, we strongly recommend that they include two dominant DISC styles and three secondary DISC styles in their job profiles.

For example, an organization who wants to hire a hunter-type salesperson might want a D- or I-style individual with D-, I- or C-secondary. Any S-style individuals would be eliminated from consideration for the role, but S-styles typically don't communicate or process information in a way that would make them successful in a hunter-type salesperson role. An S-style's preference is to work with already established processes, which is why organizations would be wise to have S-styles manage change, but not necessarily implement it.

CASE IN POINT: OVERWEIGHTED SENIOR LEADERSHIP TEAM

Juan, the CEO of an industrial company, hired us to do DISC profiles and a communication workshop for his company's senior leadership members because, in their words, "We don't know how to talk to each other." What we discovered was, of the six members of the senior leadership team, two were C-style with one of the C-styles shifting to an S-style at work, and the other four were D-styles with one, the CEO, shifting to an I-style at work, while the others shifted to be more D-style than they already were.

Within three months of our session, the senior leadership team had implemented DISC across the company. This training reduced communication conflicts to almost zero. One of the D-style senior leaders left because he saw that his communication style was no longer a good fit with the organization.

FOUR SCENARIOS OF OVERWEIGHTING AND IMPLICATIONS FOR CHANGE

1. *Overweighted Task Orientation, Underweighted People Orientation*

Occurs when: Organization is mostly D- and/or C-style.

Benefits for creating, implementing, and managing change: Because D-styles are quick to make (and unmake) decisions, deciding what, who, and when the change will happen will be easy for them. Because C-styles are comfortable with detail and process, where and how the change will happen will be easy for them. Thus, organizations overweighted with task-oriented individuals can and will create and implement change quickly.

Detriments to creating, implementing, and managing change: For D-styles the *why* of change is typically *because*, as in "because I said so." For C-styles, the *why* of change is buried under a mountain of data that indicates this change is the right one to implement. Especially for Millennials, the *why* behind the *what* is often the most important aspect of any change. However, it is typically the component that D- and C-styles spend the least amount of time on when communicating change to their team. In the case of C-styles, they lose their team somewhere between bullet 19 and 46 of their "reasons for this change" slide.

Also, because D- and C-styles typically lack people orientation, they may fail to consider the impact of change on their team. This lack of awareness can lead to increased change resistance or turnover as team members become disillusioned with a change that feels forced on them.

If this is your organization: Recruit a people-oriented

individual into your change development, implementation, and management team. As a D- or C-style leader, ask yourself, "How will my team feel about this change?" and "How can I communicate this to them in a way that makes the change relevant to them?" That last question will be addressed later in this chapter when we cover modifying communication styles.

2. *Overweighted Active Communication,*
    Underweighted Reserved Communication

Occurs when: Organization is mostly D- and/or I-style.

Benefits for creating, implementing, and managing change: D- and I-styles can energize a group either through their clear vision of the future (D-styles) or their enthusiasm for the change (I-styles). With their active communication style, D- and I-styles will be quick to execute change and, for the I-styles, can be good cheerleaders for raising spirits during a long implementation when their team starts to lose momentum.

Detriments to creating, implementing, and managing change: D-styles tend to communicate with absolute certainty (e.g., "We're going there") without making time to communicate how they and their team will get there or why they chose that mountaintop to reach. This uncertainty will terrify S-styles who fear a disruption in their status quo and annoy C-styles who need to hear and believe the details of a change before committing. In changes that take time to implement (e.g., a new software program, new telephone system or building a new office), D-styles will move on to other goals and projects before properly delegating to their team, which causes them to get pulled back in to fix implementation problems that could have been avoided.

I-styles tend to communicate with a lot of enthusiasm (e.g., "This new benefits package is going to be great!"), but, like D-styles, will forget the *how* and the *why* of the change. Because I-styles typically chase shiny objects and don't get into details, they, of all four DISC styles, are the most susceptible to creating "flavor of the month" changes that quickly wear out their team.

If this is your organization: Check and double-check your plan to ensure that you have addressed the *how* and the *why* of your change. Slow down your communication—break it into small pieces if you have time—to recruit the S- and C-style members of your organization into your change process. Address how you will support your team and the specific roadmap for change.

3. *Overweighted People Orientation, Underweighted Task Orientation*

Occurs when: Organization is mostly I- and/or S-style.

Benefits for creating, implementing, and managing change: The I-style's excitement for change combined with the S-style's supportive communication style tends to create positive responses in an organization.

Since I-styles prefer changes that are fun or exciting and S-styles prefer those that will lead to greater group harmony, they have the *who* and the *why* of change locked down, which is especially important for Millennials to understand before buying into a change.

Detriments to creating, implementing, and managing change: While they have the *who* and *why* locked down, the I-style's tendency towards chasing shiny objects and the S-style's preference for the status quo means that the *when*, *where*, *what*, and *how* of change is significantly less clear.

Changes that aren't fun or are likely to create disharmony or involve a lot of detail and disruption to established procedures will likely be avoided until they are a 90% crisis instead of a 10% crisis.

If this is your organization: Commit to non-negotiable start and completion dates for your change and create a work-back schedule with clear accountabilities and deadlines for progress. Include regular check-ins with your team members with a clear agreement up front that they are welcome to share any misgivings or grievances related to the change. In this way, you can address 10% crises before they become 90% crises.

4. *Overweighted Reserved Communication, Underweighted Active Communication*

Occurs when: Organization is mostly S- and/or C-style

Benefits for creating, implementing, and managing change: Both S- and C-styles prefer routine, so managing change with a specific process and specific milestones for success burns fewer mental calories for them.

S-styles tend to have the *who* and the *why* of change covered due to their people orientation. C-styles often have the *how* and *where* covered due to their process orientation, and, through their analysis of the need for change, they will typically have the *what* figured out as well.

Detriments to creating, implementing, and managing change: S-styles are uncomfortable with change (especially when it will impact their people), so they sometimes take an "everything's fine" approach even if the organization is crumbling around them.

As both S- and C-styles are reserved in their communication style, they can frustrate D-styles and I-styles who want them to get to the point and take action.

The reserved communication style of S-styles and C-styles also hinders them from making quick changes. They want to ensure that no one will be put out (S-styles) or that they have all information necessary to make a decision on a course of action (C-styles). This slower decision-making process may cause them to lose Millennial members of the team who prefer to make quick decisions and take action.

If this is your organization: Help team members accept that change will happen with or without them. It's better to take action with incomplete information that may cause hurt feelings in the near term than to avoid having change happen to you and dealing with the fallout of inaction later. Take small actions that build to big change, instead of waiting—and planning and analyzing and re-planning—to implement a change all at once.

Exercise: You and Your Team

Take some time to look back at you and your team. Write down how your communication styles are likely to benefit your organization when you change, how your communication styles are likely to be detrimental to a change program, and two specific actions you will take to mitigate those detriments.

Team members' dominant communication style is: D ___ I ___ S ___ C ___

How your communication styles are likely to be beneficial when you change:

_____

_____

_____

_____

How your communication styles are likely to be detrimental when you change:

_____

_____

_____

_____

Two specific actions you will take to mitigate those detriments:

1. _____

_____

_____

_____

2. _____

_____

_____

_____

MODIFYING YOUR COMMUNICATION STYLE TO CREATE BUY-IN

Just like human beings tend to hang out with people who communicate the way they do, people also tend to communicate change the way that they want change communicated to them.

The rule Sandler clients learn when discussing DISC, especially in a leadership context, is: "The one who initiates, modifies." This means that, for example, an I-style leader who wants to communicate change to a C-style team member must speak as the C-style is comfortable—logically with plenty of facts and details to satisfy the team member's need for that kind of communication.

Don't take this to mean that I-style individuals need to become C-style. Once they communicate their message, they can revert back and listen to their team members in their preferred communication style, then modify again when it's their turn to speak. This modify/revert method works best when you ask a question because you can listen to the answer in your style, ask a question in their style, then revert to your style to listen to their answer.

CASE IN POINT: ANNOUNCING A TRAINING PROGRAM

Janine, the CEO of a technology company, invited us to her office for the announcement of our training engagement with her organization. The CEO was slightly uncomfortable because her team had a lot of S- and C-style individuals who weren't prepared for this change. After a quick coaching session, Janine announced our engagement with the statement below. See if you can pick out the DISC communication styles in the announcement. (Without the benefit of tonality some parts might be tough.)

"We have engaged Sandler Training for leadership, sales, and customer service training, which will begin next month on the 10th. This is an exciting new development for our company, which will bring lots of new opportunities for us to grow and expand. Now, this won't be easy for any of us, leadership included. One of Sandler's mottos is, 'You won't fail because we won't let you.' They have built several support structures into the training to guide you and your colleagues through the training and adapt it to your world with minimal disruption to your day-to-day. I will walk you through our initial roll-out phase in detail and provide high-level details on our engagement with Sandler after roll-out is complete."

You probably caught the D...

"We have engaged Sandler Training for leadership, sales, and customer service training, which will begin next month on the 10th."

...the I...

"This is an exciting new development for our company, which will bring lots of new opportunities for us to grow and expand."

...the S...

"Now, this won't be easy for any of us, leadership included. One of Sandler's mottos is, 'You won't fail because we won't let you.' They have built several support structures into the training to guide you and your colleagues through the training and adapt it to your world with minimal disruption to your day-to-day."

...and the C:

"I will walk you through our initial roll-out phase in detail and provide high-level details on our engagement with Sandler after roll-out is complete."

By incorporating all DISC styles into her announcement, Janine communicated to everyone on the team in a way that allowed all the communication needs to be satisfied. As a result, we had significantly fewer hiccups than we would have and a smoother transition into other phases of our engagement.

LEVERAGING DISC AND CHANGE AS AN INDIVIDUAL

If you don't work with a team, you will have fewer opportunities to master the DISC designations and it may be more difficult for you to make adaptations when interacting with others (such as prospects). Remember that most people have a secondary DISC style to balance out their dominant style and, in some cases, they have two (although the tertiary style is often so low that it is almost non-existent from a communication preference perspective).

One way to round out your approach is to find a buddy. You can think of a buddy as anyone who isn't you who balances your DISC style and is open to helping you with your change. That person probably exists in your life now; it's possibly someone you have had a conflict with in the past because your communication preferences differ. If that's the case, use your knowledge of DISC to help you repair that relationship and recruit your buddy.

1. **If you are D-style**: Spend time with your buddy creating clarity around the *why* for the change. Your conviction will be much stronger if you can confidently explain your *why* to another. Once you've clarified your *why*, create a plan for how you will accomplish your change. The path to personal mountaintops is rarely as straight as one might think. Having a plan, even one that is just high-level bullet points, will help you get back on track if you stray from your path.

2. **If you are I-style:** Commit with your buddy to a specific *when* and *what* for your change. You raise your chances for success if you commit (that means "write down") a start time, a completion time, and the specific change

you will make. Like D-styles, create a strong *how* as well, with more than just bullet points, to help shield your eyes from the shiny things that will appear on your way up your mountain.

3. **If you are S-style:** Look ahead to 3, 6, 9, and 12 months from now with your buddy and determine where you want to be personally and professionally. After committing to a *where*, figure out what has to happen today to get you there, and then commit to taking one small step every day on the path up your mountain. As you take more steps, you will get uncomfortable. Keep your commitment to taking one small step per day, and you will eventually reach your mountaintop.

4. **If you are C-style:** Before diving into the *how* with your buddy, commit to a *when* for beginning and have your buddy hold you accountable to that date. Also, before getting to the *how*, create a *why* that you can share in 20 seconds or less. It is easier to recruit a buddy to help you with a change he can grasp quickly. Once you begin your path up to your mountaintop, give yourself permission to stick with your path or to adjust slightly if new information indicates a smoother path. Just make sure you don't stop moving to analyze the new data.

THIS CHAPTER IN 45 SECONDS

- DISC measures how a person likes to give and receive information. It does not measure personality or intelligence.
- People can and do communicate in each of the four DISC styles, but they have a dominant and secondary style that are most comfortable to them.

- Communicating in your dominant and secondary styles burns fewer mental calories than communicating in the other styles.
- A D-style's biggest fear is losing control.
- An I-style's biggest fear is rejection.
- An S-style's biggest fear is change.
- A C-style's biggest fear is being wrong.
- Organizations weighted with D- and C-styles can create and implement change quickly, but might lose people because they lack a *why*.
- Organizations weighted with D- and I-styles can energize a group for change, but implementation and management might fall apart from the lack of detail and delegation.
- Organizations weighted with I- and S-styles can implement and manage changes that benefit their team without creating discord, but tend to avoid changes that aren't fun, involve a lot of detail, or disrupt established procedures.
- Organizations weighted with S- and C-styles can manage change with a specific implementation process and specific progress milestones, but struggle to do it quickly.
- The one who initiates a communication should be the one to modify his style to meet the communication needs of his audience.
- As an individual, the best way to leverage your DISC style when changing is to find a buddy who complements your natural styles to provide a balancing perspective.

CHAPTER 3

Scripts and Hardwiring That Affect Change

Understanding your own "hardwired" responses to new situations, through transactional analysis, can give you tools for effectively managing your own reactions to change. In this chapter, we'll take a close look at where that hardwiring comes from and how it works.

EXERCISE: YOUR REACTIONS TO CHANGE

Rank the following statements from 1–6, with 1 being "most often" and 6 being "least often." You can't have a tie. Don't spend a lot of time thinking about your answer. This exercise is about reactions.

When someone in your life (peer, direct supervisor, spouse, partner, friend, etc.) says, "We're going to make a change," do you:

_____ Defend the status quo?

_____ Seek to understand how the change could support you and your colleagues/friends/family?

_____ Take in the information and sort through it?

_____ Go along with the change?

_____ Become excited by the thought of changing?

_____ Wonder how to undermine the change process?

We'll revisit this exercise later in the chapter.

TRANSACTIONAL ANALYSIS: INTERNAL HARDWIRING

The theory of transactional analysis (TA), first put forward by Professor Eric Byrne through his research at the University of California at Berkeley in the late 1950s and early 1960s, states that all humans have three recorders or "ego states": the Parent, the Adult, and the Child. These ego states are represented in the figure below.

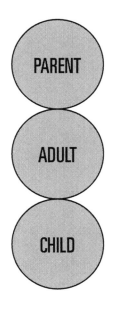

The Parent and Child ego states are split into two and three sub-ego states respectively. The Parent has a "Critical" side and a "Nurturing" side, and the Child has an "Adapted" side, a "Natural" side, and a "Little Professor" side which are shown in the following figure.

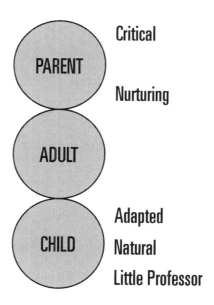

PARENT EGO STATE

The Parent ego state turns on when a person is born and shuts off at about six years old. It contains all of the messages (aka "scripts") received from parents and other authority figures (grandparents, aunts, uncles, older siblings, coaches, teachers, etc.). Once the Parent ego state shuts off, those messages live within for the rest of the person's life and can't be erased. Typically these messages are the "do's and don'ts" and "shoulds and shouldn'ts" that were learned prior to the age of six. For example, "Never talk to strangers," is a Parent script that most sales managers have to coach through when they bring on a new salesperson.

Critical Parent

Imagine an adult standing over a child, pointing his finger at the child and using sentences that include "you." For example, "Why are you so special?" and "What makes you think that anyone wants to talk to you?" Critical Parent scripts, such as "You can't," may live inside the team members with whom you need to implement and manage a change regarding your relationship.

Keep in mind that while the Parent scripts can never be erased, they can be modified and controlled.

CASE IN POINT: MOM, I LOVE YOU, BUT...

A salesperson we worked with wasn't making prospecting calls. He had been recruited by his current company based on his track record, which had been based on leveraging past relationships for introductions. In his new role, this salesperson was expected to make prospecting calls. But he wouldn't, and he was about three weeks away from being let go.

During a coaching session, he shared with us that his mother had grown up in a rough area and had escaped a kidnapping attempt when she was young after she had stopped to give someone directions in her town. From that day forward, she was extremely uncomfortable around people she didn't know. Unwittingly, she had passed a strong "never talk to strangers" script to her son.

We suggested that this salesperson have a "conversation" with his mother, who had passed several years before. We explained in a coaching session that if the salesperson really wanted to do away with this hindering script, he would need to tell his mother that while he loved her and appreciated the protection that she gave him when he was growing up, he now needed to talk to strangers to support and protect his own family.

The following week, the salesperson proudly announced that he had had that "conversation" with his mother. The following day he made two prospecting calls. While that didn't yet meet his weekly target, it was better than the zero calls he had been making before. He continued to improve.

Nurturing Parent

Imagine an adult hugging a crying child softly, saying, "It'll be OK." Someone who grew up with one or both parents who were nurturing will have scripts like, "You can do it," "If at first you don't succeed, try and try again," and "Everything works out in the end." That last one can be taken to an extreme, but the non-extreme meaning is: "Even if you feel like the world is against you, it isn't. Keep doing the right things to grow, and you will be satisfied with the final result." That script has kept me going when I've gone through massive changes in my life and felt like there would be no end to the darkness I was experiencing.

Keep in mind that while the Nurturing Parent ego state sounds positive, it can have a negative side that may manifest when nurturing turns to enabling.

CASE IN POINT: ENABLING MANAGER

Manager Sean delegated part of his change effort to Dave to implement with his peers. Dave's implementation hadn't started so Sean sought to find out why.

SEAN: Dave, thanks for coming in. I wanted to chat with you about how your implementation is going.

DAVE: Sure, Sean. I've got nothing to report.

SEAN: Oh?

DAVE: I can't get any traction with the others. They tell me to my face that they'll support me and implement the changes that I asked them to, but then they just go off and do the same things!

SEAN: Interesting. What have you done to address that?

DAVE: Nothing! I don't get why they won't listen. We've all worked together for years. We go to lunch together. We have a good time. Now I feel like they're all laughing behind my back.

SEAN: Well, I won't stand for that. Dave, let me take this implementation off your plate. I'll roll it out myself and make sure they listen to me. OK?

DAVE: That's great, Sean! Thanks so much for making me feel better.

Sean just taught Dave that whenever he runs into a problem (this situation is internal, but Dave's brain won't record it that way), he can run to Sean and Sean will handle it for him. Sean has to learn that he just cost himself his most valuable resource—his time—from this one incident.

ADULT EGO STATE

The Adult ego state turns on when people begin to be independent from their parents, usually when they start crawling. The Adult runs for the rest of one's life. It is best envisioned as a computer that takes in information, decides what ego state should handle that information, and activates the appropriate response.

For example, your colleague asks, "What time is it?" Your Adult takes in that information, decides that it is an information-only request, and activates an Adult response, "It's around 8:30."

The Adult also controls those Parent and Child ego states, which can never be erased. However, sometimes a person can be Parent- or Child-affected, which means a sub-ego state of the Parent or Child is dominant over that person's Adult.

Revisiting the above example, your colleague says, "What time is it?" The Critical-Parent–affected individual responds, "Time to get a watch." The Little-Professor–affected individual says, "Wouldn't you like to know?"

Typically being Parent- or Child-affected isn't positive. The individual will be either highly judgmental of change (Critical Parent), overly accommodating (Adapted Child), or likely to sabotage through passive-aggressive resistance (Little Professor).

The best way to bring someone out of their Parent or Child ego state is to stay in your Adult, ask questions, and restate what you hear. We'll cover this more later when we look at games people play while changing and how to end those games.

CASE IN POINT: MANAGING A PARENT- OR CHILD-AFFECTED INDIVIDUAL

Susan's peer Albert wanted to vent to her about a recent change to vacation approvals, which used to be managed team-by-team on a spreadsheet. Now everyone had to use the company intranet to request and approve vacation.

ALBERT: This is totally ludicrous, Susan!

SUSAN: What is, Albert?

ALBERT: This stupid new vacation approval system.

SUSAN: Because?

ALBERT: Because I've got enough to do without having to log into our terrible intranet to approve my team's vacation days. It used to be simple when I used a spreadsheet!

SUSAN: I understand. If you had a magic wand what would you do?

ALBERT: I'd go back to the spreadsheet. It was way easier for me.

SUSAN: That's fair. What happens when one of your team members is working with another group and that group doesn't know about your team member's vacation?

ALBERT: Huh. I figured that person would tell them.

SUSAN: I'm sure he would, but people forget sometimes. Is that fair to say?

ALBERT: That's fair.

SUSAN: So how can I support you in getting comfortable with the new vacation system?

> ALBERT: Got 10 minutes to walk me through it?
>
> SUSAN: Not right now, but how about Thursday or Friday? Which is better for you?
>
> ALBERT: Friday morning. We usually arrive at the same time. How about then?
>
> SUSAN: I can make that work. Would you send me a meeting invite?
>
> ALBERT: Absolutely. Thanks for letting me vent.

By staying in her Adult ego state, Susan allowed Albert to shift out of his Critical Parent and come to an Adult conclusion that using the new system was better for the company even if he had to suffer through a brief period of discomfort to change his behavior.

CHILD EGO STATE

Like the Parent ego state, the Child ego state turns on when a person is born and shuts off at about six years old. The emotional reactions to the messages stored in the Parent ego state are locked in the Child ego state.

The Child state is where one's sense of compliance, need for approval, sense of humor, and sense of fear live. It is the seat of both mischief and anger.

Adapted Child

The Adapted Child could also be called the "Compliant Child." When someone makes a request and your first reaction is, "Yes, right away!," you are operating from your Adapted Child ego state.

The Adapted Child also contains your need for approval, which can lead you to go along with change that doesn't benefit you or potentially even hurts you. The Adapted Child just wants to be liked.

CASE IN POINT: WHO ARE YOU, REALLY?

As a child, Brian was told, "Be a nice boy. You want people to like you." As Brian grew up, the Adapted Child script that had been planted in him prompted him to try recreational drugs because his friends pressured him, adopt a vegan diet to please his girlfriend, join a gym because he wanted to fit in at work, and take classes in subjects he really didn't care for because his parents implied he should. Brian's identity was tied up in changing into what he thought others said he should be instead of being what he believed he could be.

Natural Child

Your parents didn't have to teach you how to laugh or play. You were born with those scripts inside your Natural Child. Your parents or your environment did teach you how to be afraid. Your sense of joy and sense of fear both live in your Natural Child ego state.

When you feel yourself getting really excited about creating change, that's your Natural Child. When you feel yourself fearing the unknown as you contemplate implementing it, that's your Natural Child, too.

Leading change will require you to effectively manage your Natural Child ego state. If you are too exuberant, you will reduce buy-in from your team members who feel you are being unrealistic about the time or effort required. If you are too afraid, you will start your company down the path to failure.

Little Professor/Rebellious Child

The Little Professor is the Child's version of the Adult ego state. It typically manifests itself as mischief or passive-aggressive behavior.

Little-Professor–affected leaders implement change because they get their needs met watching their employees try and fail to meet their ever-changing expectations.

Employees who are Little-Professor–affected will play games with their leaders during implementation and management because they get their needs met by upsetting others. Escaping a Little Professor's game requires staying in your Adult ego state, as the following Case in Point describes.

CASE IN POINT: MANAGING A LITTLE-PROFESSOR–AFFECTED EMPLOYEE

Shen's direct report Carl won't enter data into the customer relationship management (CRM) program her company rolled out three months before despite completing training and receiving extra coaching when requested. Shen needs data from each direct report to complete quarterly reporting to the executive team. This is the third conversation she and Carl have had about missing data since he completed training on the database.

SHEN: Carl, I need your help. My quarterly reporting is due at the end of next week. I need your data to be in the CRM by next Wednesday so I can pull my reports. When I checked yesterday, you hadn't entered anything for this quarter.

CARL: Oh yeah. Slipped my mind. Don't worry about it, Shen.

SHEN: Thanks for letting me know, Carl. My sense is there's a disconnect between you and the CRM. Is that fair to say?

CARL: Not really.

SHEN: Well, what would be fair?

CARL: What's with all the pressure, Shen? The CRM's pretty easy to use. I can probably bang in my data for the quarter in 45 minutes.

SHEN: Just 45 minutes? That's great, Carl. Let's look at your calendar and find a 45-minute block between now and next Wednesday when you can get your data entered. I'll make sure you aren't interrupted.

CARL: Uh, OK. How about Monday between 9:00 and 10:00?

SHEN: Works for me, Carl. May I ask you one more thing?

CARL: Sure...

SHEN (gently): Let's say that your data isn't entered by 10:00 on Monday. What would you like me to do?

CARL: You won't have to do anything. I'll make sure to get it done.

> SHEN: Glad to hear it. How about we set aside some time next week to figure out a system that works for you for entering data so we don't have to have this conversation again?
> CARL: I'd like that.
> SHEN: Great. Since you've got your calendar out already...

Games start when someone "discounts," which usually sounds like, "Don't worry," or something similar. Carl discounted Shen's question about data and then became angry when she called his game by using "my sense is...fair to say?" By staying in her Adult ego state and asking questions instead of reacting to Carl's emotions, Shen pulled information out of Carl (45 minutes to enter data) that he might not have revealed otherwise, then used that information to help Carl come up with his own solution.

While that scene is brief, in a real-world interaction, Shen may have had to ask four or more Adult questions to pull Carl out of his Little Professor ego state.

Exercise: Revisiting Your Reactions to Change

Revisiting the exercise from the beginning of the chapter, label the statements with their corresponding ego state.

_____ Defend the status quo

_____ Seek to understand how the change could support you and your colleagues/friends/family

_____ Take in the information and sort through it

_____ Go along with the change

_____ Become excited by the thought of changing

_____ Wonder how to undermine the change process

The first statement relates to the Critical Parent, the second to the Nurturing Parent, the third to the Adult, the fourth to the Adapted Child, the fifth to the Natural Child, and the sixth to the Little Professor.

REACTING OR RESPONDING TO CHANGE

When you face a change in your life, you can either react or respond. When you react, typically it's by accessing the Critical Parent or Child ego states. When you respond, you are accessing the Adult state to choose the best ego state to communicate, which could be the Critical Parent or one of the Child sub-ego states.

The concept of "react or respond" is critical to keep in mind when communicating change to another person or a group. Humans are hardwired to be risk averse. That's how cities and societies came to be. Enough shared ancestors decided to be safe rather than investigating that strange rustling noise in the bushes.

Expect that most people with whom you share your proposed change will react instead of respond. To prevent things from being derailed, you must be emotionally unattached from the outcome of your communication. If you're emotionally invested in your audience vociferously accepting the proposed change, you'll likely end up disappointed and what you proposed will probably end there.

You may be inclined to focus on the Critical Parent ego state when thinking about your audience's reaction. However, the Child reactions can be just as damaging to implementation and management, especially Little Professor and Natural Child. Don't concern yourself with the Adapted Child because this ego state seeks to please. A reaction from the Adapted Child will appear as compliance.

Little Professor reactions will, on the surface, appear supportive. However, the actions of individuals reacting from their Little Professor will demonstrate that they are actually sabotaging. You may also hear verbal eye-rolling, such as, "Yeah, I'm sure that's going to work."

If your audience reacts from the fear side of their Natural Child, that will likely manifest from their Critical Parent. When children are afraid, they typically seek comfort from their parent. If parents feel their child is in danger, they will lash out to protect.

If your audience reacts from the play side of their Natural Child, they will initially be excited and willing. The danger with this reaction is when your audience feels the process has become boring. Keeping your process engaging and interesting to your audience will be key for a successful implementation.

COMBINING DISC AND TA TO IDENTIFY CHANGE CHALLENGES

C Adult / Critical Parent	Critical Parent / Adult **D**
S Nurturing Parent / Adapted Child	Natural Child / Little Professor **I**

Understanding how each DISC style likes to give and receive information will help you communicate change more effectively.

By laying the filter of TA over DISC, you can identify potential challenges implementing and managing your change.

Because of their preference for achievement and difficulty understanding those that can't or won't achieve like they do, the ego state of D-styles tends to be Critical Parent. D-style individuals also prefer high-level facts, which makes their secondary ego state their Adult.

With I-styles' preference for fun, their style ego state tends to be Natural Child. When I-styles feel like they aren't getting their needs met, they will switch into Little Professor.

As they tend to be the most nurturing communicators of the four DISC styles, S-styles' default ego state is the Nurturing Parent. Because S-styles fear disharmony in their group, they will fall into the Adapted Child ego state if they sense that going along with the crowd will keep their group together.

The C-style's primary ego state is the Adult, but C-styles will switch into Critical Parent when they want to prove how smart they are or when they get frustrated with an individual who "doesn't get it."

Don't take the DISC/TA tie-in as an absolute. An individual's preferred ego state has a lot to do with their first six years of life when their Parent and Child scripts are running. For example, someone can be D-style with a preferred ego state of Nurturing Parent if he had an incredibly nurturing mother or father.

Taking DISC and TA into account, let's look at how your scripting may impede successful implementation of your new initiative and how to minimize the effects of your team members' scripting as you plan, implement, and manage change.

1. **D-style leader (Critical Parent/Adult):** Your Critical Parent will make you want your change to have been done yesterday so look for small positive indications that your team is implementing it. Leverage your Adult to define clear outcomes and milestones, but remember that most of your team responds better to emotions than hard numbers.

   What to do when you have D-style direct reports: Enlist them in creating personal milestones for your change and potentially being a devil's advocate for you prior to rolling it out to the entire team. If you choose the devil's advocate option, ensure that you clearly define the box in which your reports can perform this role. Be clear to them that change is going to happen to reduce the potential for your report to undermine it when you roll it out.

2. **I-style leader (Natural Child/Little Professor):** Your Natural Child can promote excitement in your team, but it could also cause you to become fearful of what you and your team need to do to complete your change. If you feel like offering incentives (tangible or intangible) after implementation to motivate your employees, that is your Little Professor seeking to play games with your team.

   What to do when you have I-style direct reports: Only share as much as necessary for your reports to understand what they are supposed to do next, and then celebrate that small victory. If you sense game playing, have a private meeting with your report and use the questioning strategy outlined under the "Little Professor" section of this chapter.

3. **S-style leader (Nurturing Parent/Adapted Child):** Be completely clear with your team members about their accountabilities when implementing and managing your change, or your negative Nurturing Parent will cause you to take on your team's work as your own. At some point in the middle, your Adapted Child may cause you to think about stopping it. Developing a clear idea of where you want to be personally and professionally, which is in Chapter 2: *DISCussing Change,* will mostly eliminate your Adapted Child from appearing.

   What to do when you have S-style direct reports: Bring your S-style team members on board when you are planning your change, and ask them to help you determine how to nurture it from implementation through management and completion. If you are clear that it will happen, you can leverage their Adapted Child to create compliance.

4. **C-style leader (Adult/Critical Parent):** You'll likely have a step-by-step plan created for implementing and managing change with clear outcomes and milestones that will overwhelm the I- and S-styles on your team. This may frustrate you and prompt you to take on all of the work yourself. Before taking over a task from one of your team members, be curious about the gap between what you think you

said and what they heard. You'll find that that approach ends up being less work for you.

What to do when you have C-style direct reports: Be prepared to answer a ton of questions from your *why* to the *why now* to your implementation plan to your outcomes and milestones. Remind your C-style team members to stay focused on the end result and avoid majoring in the minor details.

THIS CHAPTER IN 45 SECONDS

- Transactional analysis (TA) is the theory of how humans interact.
- The Parent ego state turns on when a person is born and shuts off at about six years old. It contains all of the "shoulds" and "should nots" from parents and other authority figures during these early years.
- The Child ego state turns on when a person is born and shuts off at about six years old. It contains emotional reactions to the messages stored in our Parent ego state.
- Parent and Child messages stay with people for the rest of their lives and can never be erased.
- The Adult ego state turns on when people start to become independent from their parents, usually when they begin crawling, and runs for the rest of their lives.
- The Adult ego state is a computer that takes information in and decides what to do with it, including accessing the Parent or Child ego states.
- When you face a change, you have a choice to react or respond.

- Reacting typically means lashing out through the Parent (Critical) or Child ego states.

- Responding typically means using the Adult ego state to determine the best response, which may mean accessing the Critical Parent or Child.

- Laying TA on top of DISC helps you understand how each DISC style reacts or responds.

- A D-style's ego state tends to be Critical Parent followed by Adult.

- An I-style's ego state tends to be Natural Child followed by Little Professor.

- An S-style's ego state tends to be Nurturing Parent followed by Adapted Child.

- A C-style's ego state tends to be Adult followed by Critical Parent.

- Individuals' DISC style and preferred ego states can be affected by their upbringing.

CHAPTER 4

Angels, Agnostics, and Atheists

A nyone who has experienced change with a group has witnessed these three factions: angels, agnostics, and atheists.

The angels are change champions. They buy into it immediately and fervently work to implement it.

Agnostics are change observers. They believe that change might be good, but they aren't convinced so they will wait on the edge and observe. If implementation goes well, the agnostics will become angels. If it goes poorly or runs into a significant roadblock, the agnostics will become atheists.

Atheists are change deniers. They don't believe that a change, this change, or any change is right, now or in the future. Atheists fall into two camps: the first group works quietly to undermine your change effort while appearing to be agnostic on the surface.

The second group is vocal, loud, and destructive because they may paralyze some of your angels as well as sway your agnostics.

As a rule of thumb, the split of angels, agnostics, and atheists tends to be 20%, 60%, 20% respectively. For easy math, an organization of 100 individuals will have 20 angels, 60 agnostics, and 20 atheists (give or take a few in each category).

The number of angels and atheists will adjust based on the type of change, stealing from the number of agnostics. In a change that most in the organization can generally agree on (e.g., "casual Fridays"), there will be more angels and fewer atheists. In one that most in the organization don't appreciate (e.g., moving from a defined benefit to a defined contribution pension plan), there will be fewer angels and more atheists.

CASE IN POINT: NEW BONUS PLAN

An oilfield service company planned to introduce variable compensation into the bonus plan for the operations team. Up to this point, this team had been paid a quarterly bonus based on overall company performance, which was largely outside team members' control.

The new bonus plan would reduce the amount of guaranteed compensation, but the overall potential quarterly bonus was bigger. Unsurprisingly, the HR manager and CEO had few angels to lean on. The operations workers, who weren't unionized, quickly bonded around a shared goal of stopping this new compensation plan.

Fortunately for the HR manager and CEO, they

understood how to communicate with the operators based on DISC styles and were able to draw a line to the new bonus plan that helped employees achieve their personal goals.

When the new plan was rolled out, several operators left the company, but they were quickly replaced. Under the new plan, the managers paid out more to their operators in bonuses, but they balanced that additional expense with reducing costs from lost time due to injuries and increased productivity in their remaining team.

Traditional change management techniques focus on getting the atheists on board, which is a waste of time for both leader and employee. Traditionally trained managers also tend to take their angels for granted because angels give overt support through their words and behavior. However, angels will become agnostics if the support is not returned by their leader.

Exercise: Your Angels, Agnostics, and Atheists

Sticking as close to the 20/60/20 rule as possible, think of a recent change initiative and split your team into angels, agnostics, and atheists. (You may want to use first names or initials only.)

Angels

_____

_____

_____

_____

Agnostics

_____

_____

_____

_____

Atheists

_____

_____

_____

_____

If you found this was a difficult exercise, you're not alone. Leaders who work with Sandler typically struggle to split up their team when one or more categories don't have a positive connotation. Putting one member of your team in the "atheist" category doesn't mean he is a bad person or a bad fit for the organization. He may be one of your top performers, but he also might be one of your biggest obstacles to implementing your change.

CASE IN POINT: I FEEL LIKE A PEDDLER

An industrial service company hired Frankie, a salesperson with a mandate to service clients and upsell products or services that were a good fit for them. This salesperson quickly developed a great rapport with the client base, but sales to existing clients didn't increase. It turned out that inbound leads simply weren't being acted on.

His leader gave him multiple chances to succeed, including coaching and training to sell more effectively. Frustrated by seeing no change in the salesperson, the leader asked what was preventing him from doing his job. The salesperson's response was, "I feel like a peddler." This kind of remark was typical; it signaled a personal refusal to move out of the comfort zone that could be called "classic atheist."

Frankie was let go shortly after that exchange. Sales in his territory increased by over $100,000 in each of the months immediately following his termination because the individual who replaced him, who wasn't a salesperson, actually performed the behavior the leader expected.

WORKING WITH ANGELS

Angels can be D-, I-, S-, or C-style. What all angels have in common is they quickly comprehend a) why the change is good for their organization and b) why it will be good for them. The "quickly" part is what separates an angel from an agnostic. Agnostics might become angels, but they need time to accept that the change is good for their organization or for them.

Angels tend to be driven by their Natural Child (excitement) or Nurturing Parent (supporting others) ego states. When you communicate with your angels, focus first on activating their Natural Child. Just like a human child, the Child ego state is the part of people that says, "I want that." Then they go recruit their

Parent and Adult to make "that" happen. In our context, "that" is the change you're communicating with them.

LEVERAGING ANGELS PRE-CHANGE

To test if you have an angel on your team, have an individual conversation with each team member about a change that might happen—not literally in those words, but whatever words work for you to test your team members' reactions. If they enthusiastically jump on board, possibly asking questions for clarity, you probably have an angel.

Once your angels are identified, include them in pre-implementation planning as much as you can or are allowed legally. Even inclusion in seemingly trivial meetings demonstrates your trust in your angels and reinforces their commitment to executing your change successfully.

Including angels in pre-implementation planning may sound exclusionary. It is. There is zero benefit in including agnostics and atheists in your planning sessions aside from slowing down and potentially killing your change. Angels earn the privilege of being included in planning by supporting the leader from the beginning. Agnostics and atheists can earn similar privileges if they become angels, but they should always be excluded from the beginning stages of planning.

LEVERAGING ANGELS ON IMPLEMENTATION

Because they aren't you, angels have more opportunity to grow support for the change from the base of your organization. It's similar to how children will obey a suggestion their grandparent makes that the parents had made several times with no results.

Change begins by breaking the inertia of your current status quo. Leverage the forward momentum that angels have already through their pre-change excitement to build momentum.

CASE IN POINT: ANGELS IN THE CRM

A communication services company planned to implement a national CRM strategy to replace the multiple CRMs in various states of disuse across the organization. Leaders identified tech-savvy, ambitious individuals across the company and enrolled them in a beta program. As the beta program neared completion, the testers were encouraged to share their experiences with their colleagues in group meetings and privately.

Instead of the usual adoption rate of 14% during final CRM rollout, 82% of potential users began and continued using the new CRM.

LEVERAGING ANGELS ON MANAGING YOUR CHANGE

Like a rechargeable battery, an angel's energy and enthusiasm for your change will run out if you, the leader, aren't recharging them. Recharging your angels comes through giving them "strokes."

A stroke is a psychological unit of interaction between two people. Strokes can be positive (e.g., "You're a great asset to this team"), negative (e.g., "You can't do anything right") or like a rubber band snapping back, which starts positive but ends negative (e.g., "I knew you'd figure it out—eventually"). Strokes are either conditional (based on performance) or unconditional (just because that person exists).

Every human requires a certain number of strokes per day. David Sandler called this the "psychological stroke counter" or PSC. The PSC resets every night, and a person then seeks to fill it each day with positive strokes.

Like a child who acts out to get attention, adults who don't get their PSC filled with positive strokes will act out to achieve their daily quota through negative strokes. In a salesperson, acting out might mean not entering data into the CRM until reprimanded by the leader.

Some people need lots of strokes to fill their PSC each day, and some need just a few, but if an individual's PSC isn't filled with positive strokes, he will seek negative strokes to reach his daily need. Think of that child who gets attention from a parent by misbehaving. The stroke is negative (e.g., "Stop that!"), but it still gets noted in the child's PSC.

The three types of strokes that recharge your angels most are:

- Written: A handwritten note, even on a sticky note, recharges an emotional battery more than anything electronic because your team member sees that you took the time to physically write instead of fire off an email. Written strokes don't need to be long or flowery. A simple "I really appreciate your help with implementing the CRM program" may be enough, or you can add specific examples if you're writing to a C-style employee or an exclamation point (implying excitement) if you're writing to an I-style employee.

- Verbal: Your choice of public or private verbal praise will depend on your employee's DISC style. For an S-style employee, being put on a stage in front of other employees and publicly praised will likely cause embarrassment and demotivation; however, if you stop briefly at the person's desk and say, "You're really supporting the team—thank you," that will give a boost to keep going. On the other hand, a D-style employee would love to be publicly praised, especially if individuals with power (executives, board members, politicians, etc.) are present.

- Time: Your most valuable possession as a leader provides the greatest recharge for your angels. Spending extra time, as little as five minutes, with your angels working on a challenge specific to them keeps their motivation going because they will draw a connection between supporting your change and accessing more of your time.

Beware of Fallen Angels

You may be unfortunate enough to encounter a fallen angel. Fallen angels play psychological games to get their needs met. This person may initially seem beneficial; however, once the fallen angel receives the psychological payoff or if the needs aren't met, that person will convert to an agnostic or atheist.

We'll address games in more detail later in this chapter, but we'll share the games fallen angels play now.

Hero

The hero has two versions: one typically played by a leader and one typically played by a fallen angel. Fallen angel heroes appear during planning or management when they are asked to help create a solution to a problem on which the rest of their team is stuck. Once these supposed angels create a solution, alone or with a team, they position their solution as completely obvious (e.g., "Why couldn't you think of this?") albeit often unsaid. By making their colleagues, including possibly their leader, feel lesser than themselves, they get their needs met and add to their PSC.

Even a leader may qualify as a fallen angel playing the hero game if he sets up his team for failure by withholding information or leaving out steps. After repeated failures, the leader steps in with a spoken or implied, "See, I'm the only one who could make this happen."

Happy-to-Help

A fallen angel who plays happy-to-help is usually the first to volunteer for a task and readily accepts additional assignments. They are setting up a "you owe me" conversation with the leader. Happy-to-help fallen angels are difficult to spot because they are so amiable. Their game might not be concluded for some time after your change effort is completed.

CASE IN POINT: THE HAPPY-TO-HELP PAYOFF

Mark met with his leader Stephanie. Nine months prior, Mark had been a part of the team that successfully implemented a just-in-time delivery process for their clients.

MARK: Thanks for seeing me, Stephanie.

STEPHANIE: No problem, Mark. What's up?

MARK: Well, I saw the internal posting for that director role, and I wanted to talk about filling it.

STEPHANIE: Oh, OK.

MARK: You see, I feel that I'd be really good in that role with all my experience and what I've done for the company recently.

STEPHANIE: Thanks for sharing. When you say, "what I've done for the company," what do you mean?

MARK: I implemented the just-in-time delivery process, and I'm always volunteering for extra assignments.

STEPHANIE: Hm. To say that "you" implemented the JIT process might be a bit of a stretch, Mark. Weren't there others involved?

MARK: Well, yeah. David, Sean, and Diane helped, but I did most of the work.

STEPHANIE: Mark, my sense is that the director role and your participation in the JIT process team aren't the real issues. Is that fair?

MARK: Stephanie, if you aren't going to support my career, then I guess I'll have to start looking elsewhere.

STEPHANIE: Mark, this is very out of character for you.

MARK: Listen, I took on a lot of extra work that I didn't need to do to get that JIT process going, and I want to be recognized for it.

STEPHANIE: Help me understand "recognized," Mark. You and the team were publicly recognized internally and externally to our clients.

MARK: That's all well and good, but I want more.

> STEPHANIE: More?
>
> MARK: Like that director role and the salary increase and benefits that come with it.
>
> STEPHANIE: Mark, do you feel that this is the best way to approach that?
>
> MARK: It's what I want.
>
> STEPHANIE (gently): Mark, that wasn't my question. Do you feel that this is the best way for you to approach positioning yourself for that director role?
>
> MARK: Um...I guess not. Sorry.

Stephanie successfully stayed out of Mark's game by not responding to Mark's emotional statements and by asking questions, which gives Mark's Adult ego state time to override his Critical Parent and Child. Getting out of games will be explored in detail later in the chapter.

CONVERTING AGNOSTICS TO ANGELS

Think of agnostics as a "moveable middle." That 60% of your organization could become atheists or angels. You, their leader, will determine which way they go and how many go that way through your actions and how you leverage your angels.

It would be nice if the entire group of agnostics would convert to angels, but some of them will become atheists as your change effort moves from implementation through management. Being prepared for that eventuality and having a plan to replace those team members will be a key part of your strategy.

If you leave your agnostics alone during pre-change planning because they won't be engaged enough, you could find that they switch to atheists if they are given too much information before buy-in.

Agnostics can also be D-, I-, S- or C-style. What is common to all agnostics no matter their DISC profile is that they desire evidence that this particular change will be better than any other change. As they notice that you are investing more time with the angels, they will be curious about how they could become part of that group.

Agnostics live on the fear side of their Natural Child ego state, the flip side to the joyful Natural Child in which your angels reside. The following steps for converting agnostics to angels are all based on minimizing or eliminating their fear of change.

FOUR STEPS TO SUCCESSFUL CONVERSION

Step One

First, you as a leader must show unwavering support for your change and communicate a crystal-clear vision for the reasons you selected it and the benefits to your people once it has been fully implemented.

Agnostics look for hesitation in their leader to reinforce their belief that this change isn't better than any other change. Planting your feet and staying true to your vision for the end result, adjusting as necessary along the way, will convert some of your agnostics to angels because they will buy into your belief that it is the right one for your organization.

A leader's number one priority, especially during the change, is to create clarity for the team. Any ambiguity about where you are, where you're going, and how you are going to get there gives your agnostics a reason to hold back their commitment.

Step Two

Second, show agnostics that the change has already been successful in a beta setting (e.g., the CRM case from earlier in this chapter) and help them understand how to apply the successes from your beta group to their world.

Under stress, humans tend to become linear thinkers. If agnostics can't draw a direct line between the change and a benefit to them, they will continue to withhold their commitment. Part of this step then is forcing your agnostics into the exploration stage of change. During this step, many leaders will feel the urge to tell their agnostics how to apply the successes of the beta group to their world. That results in more resistance instead of exploration.

CASE IN POINT: AGNOSTICS EXPLORE IMPLEMENTING A SALES PROCESS

The leader of a sales team at a transportation company planned to implement a new defined sales process to help her team work smarter and create a common language across the organization to improve customer service. Two of her highest performing salespeople were open to the idea of a new process but weren't comfortable with the process applying to them.

During a meeting with the entire sales team, the leader helped those two salespeople understand that they were essentially following a process already. It just hadn't been clearly defined for the rest of the group. Because the leader made following the sales process about the other salespeople instead of about them, one of the salespeople committed to following the process and coaching new members of the team. The other continued with a "wait and see" approach, which frustrated the leader. However, after the leader showed that salesperson how he was falling behind the rest of the sales team who was following her sales process, he came around.

Step Three

Third, leverage your angels. This step tends to make leaders uncomfortable because they interpret "leverage" to mean "have them shill for me." To paraphrase a Sandler Rule, always keep them OK. "Them" in this case is both angels and agnostics.

Keeping your angels OK means that you need to be clear from the time you approach potential angels about joining the pre-change planning or beta group that an expectation of group membership is speaking to their peers about their experiences. This peer communication includes negative experiences. No transformational change, especially one that involves humans, will go exactly to plan so make it OK for your angels to discuss experiences that are less than positive, after addressing the issues with you first. It will make them sound like less of a salesperson to your agnostics.

Keeping your agnostics OK means not selling your change to them through their peers or you. Let your agnostics gain buy-in by helping them explore how the change will benefit them.

Step Four

There's a fourth step to converting agnostics: momentum. As your change begins to take hold, savvy agnostics will support it because they believe that any change would be good and, based on the momentum you and your angels built, any change becomes this change. Those agnostics who wait until it has lots of momentum will eventually become angels, supporting by not resisting and by doing the minimum to be compliant with new behavior expectations.

Exercise: Converting Your Agnostics

Looking back at the team members you identified as potential agnostics earlier in the chapter, what is the best way to convert them to angels? Be specific with your action steps:

_____

_____

_____

_____

AVOIDING THE ATHEIST TIME SINK

Traditionally leaders waste most of their time by either cajoling their atheists to commit or ignoring them and hoping that "they'll come around." Neither behavior will make your change effort simpler or easier.

Atheists also fear change, but unlike agnostics who are willing to listen or explore how it might benefit them, their Critical Parent reacts by planting their feet in the status quo. As an atheist observes that his Critical Parent rants are effective, his Little Professor engages in game playing. Atheists play games to disrupt your efforts and get their emotional needs met, which happens best if change doesn't happen so they can stay in the status quo.

There are five common games atheists play to get their needs met during transformative change.

Watch Everybody Fight

Despite best efforts by leaders to create clarity with their teams, disconnects will happen. An atheist uses these disconnects (e.g., entering all data into the new CRM system or entering everything but pricing because Accounting isn't connected yet) to cause conflict between two peers or between a team member and the leader. The emotional payoff happens when the other parties start arguing.

Look How Hard I'm Trying

An atheist appears to comply with new behavior expectations (e.g., entering all vacation requests through the intranet vacation request program), but consistently misses a step, which causes delays and sucks the leader's time. When the leader addresses the behavior with the atheist, he claims, "Look how hard I'm trying."

If It Weren't for You

This one is a favorite of high-performing atheists. This game puts the blame for the lack of performance back on the leader.

CASE IN POINT: I'D SELL MORE IF ONLY . . .

Jason's company implemented a CRM system six months ago. He attended all of the required training but still wasn't using the system. Jason was a top-three performer on his team, but his sales dipped in the prior two months. Darryl, Jason's leader, wanted to understand what was behind the dip in performance.

DARRYL: Jason, your sales dipped the last two months, and I don't see many opportunities in the CRM that will help you make up the gap before the end of the quarter. Would you help me understand what you plan to do to hit your numbers this month and make up the gap, so you hit your quarterly target, too?

JASON: Well, if I didn't have to use that flippin' CRM, I could go out and sell more! Instead, I'm chained to my desk doing data entry!

Jason gets his emotional needs met by dumping responsibility back on Darryl.

Ain't It Awful

The quieter version of "if it weren't for you," an atheist playing "ain't it awful" wants two payoffs. One can come from a peer, or both can come from the leader.

Let's revisit Jason from our last example, first with a colleague and second with Darryl.

CASE IN POINT: AIN'T IT AWFUL I CAN'T SELL MORE

Jason discussed his lack of sales with his colleague, Tanya.

JASON: I'm really taking a beating these last two months. I can probably hit my number this month, but hitting my quarterly number will be tough. I wish I didn't have to take so much time entering stuff into our CRM.

TANYA: That's terrible, Jason. Have you spoken to Darryl?

Tanya gives Jason his emotional payoff with a version of "Ah, it is awful."

CASE IN POINT: I WISH I DIDN'T HAVE TO…

Jason and Darryl had an "ain't it awful" conversation about his sales results.

DARRYL: Jason, your sales dipped the last two months, and I don't see many opportunities in the CRM that will help you make up the gap before the end of the quarter. Would you help me understand what you plan to do to hit your numbers this month and make up the gap, so you hit your quarterly target, too?

JASON: I can probably hit my number this month, Darryl, but hitting my quarterly number will be tough. I wish I didn't have to take so much time entering stuff into our CRM.

DARRYL: Sounds like you're under a lot of pressure,

> Jason. How about you focus on making up your numbers
> and you can enter the data into our CRM at the end of the
> quarter?

In the second payoff, Darryl is giving Jason permission
to duck accountability for entering data into their CRM.
Atheists who have been with your organization for several
years will seek that payoff because they prefer to stay in their
current comfort zone. Make your change effort excuse-proof,
and you'll eliminate the opportunity for your veterans to play
"ain't it awful."

Cops and Robbers

In this game, team members consistently avoid doing expected
behavior (e.g., filing health benefit claims online) or providing
information at expected times (e.g., submitting progress reports
for installation of new equipment). The emotional payoff comes
from "hooking" the leader into confronting them about not
meeting expectations.

ESCAPING GAMES

To escape all of these games use these eight steps.

1. Assess the behaviors or words that "hook" your Critical
   Parent or Child, causing you to get trapped in a game.
2. Recognize the sense that something isn't right is your
   Parent or Child tape getting hooked.
3. Recognize from which ego state your employee is speaking.

If you feel he is reacting to your proposed change, he is communicating from his Critical Parent or Child.

4. Call the game by asking straight questions (e.g., "If you were me, what would you do?").

5. Use active listening, but avoid paraphrasing since your interpretation of your employee's words could cause a new game to begin.

6. Ask the game player to sum up what you just said—it gives his Adult time to catch up.

7. Be assertive. If you feel it, say it (gently).

8. Avoid discounting (i.e., minimizing or dismissing). Remember:

    a. *The real problem.* The problem your employee brings you is never the real problem.

    b. *The significance of the problem.* What may be insignificant to you could be critical to your employee.

    c. *The solvability of the problem.* Externalizing traps you in his game.

    d. *Your ability to solve the problem.* Giving up won't help you or your employee.

THIS CHAPTER IN 45 SECONDS

-   During change, your employees will become angels (champions), agnostics (observers), or atheists (deniers).

-   As a percentage of your team, angels, agnostics, and atheists tend to split 20/60/20.

-   Traditional leaders waste their time attempting to convert atheists, who will likely never accept any change.

-   Invest most of your time with your angels.

- Invest the rest of your time with your agnostics to attempt conversion to angels.
- Fallen angels can have ulterior motives for supporting your change.
- Agnostics need support exploring how the change would benefit them to convert to angels.
- Some agnostics will never become angels, but they might become fallen angels when they accept that your change is inevitable.
- Atheists play games to get their emotional needs met because they can't stop your change.

CHAPTER 5

Success or Failure for Change Rests with the Leader

S uccess or failure of your change effort rests solely on the shoulders of you, the leader. If this makes you uncomfortable, you might not be ready to ask your team to make the transition because you may eventually abandon them through excuses and finger pointing. In a new initiative, as the popular saying has it, "There are no bad employees, only bad leaders."

That rule doesn't mean you're a bad person, but that ultimate accountability resides with the leader. If your team isn't implementing or managing your change effectively, that is because you didn't say or do what was needed for your team to understand, believe, and execute it.

CASE IN POINT: SILENCE IS AGREEMENT AND UNDERSTANDING, RIGHT?

The vice president of sales for a communications company held a meeting with the entire sales team to share the company's revised compensation structure for the following calendar year.

After spending 50 minutes of a 60-minute meeting walking through the new compensation plan point-by-point, the vice president said, "Any questions?"

Hearing none after less than 10 seconds, he wrapped up the meeting with, "If you do have questions, there are documents on the intranet that you can review with your manager."

Within three months, salespeople who represented 42% of the previous year's net new business left that company even though they would have been impacted the least by the new compensation structure.

The vice president of sales would have been more successful with rolling out his change if he had heeded another Sandler Rule: "People buy emotionally and justify their decisions intellectually." Setting up a change means accounting for and strategizing to mitigate the inevitable emotional involvement of your team.

It's easy for leaders to rush into implementation and management. This drive can be great if they are leading themselves through a simple personal change. It's not so great, though, if the change is more complex and involves more people than choosing water over a soda at lunch.

A leader's role in change is to interpret the change for team members so they can transition effectively, to communicate the reasons for the change, and to enable the team to succeed by providing the tools and support necessary. Exceptional leaders perform this role through the permission, protection, and potency they give each team member.

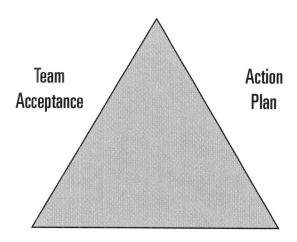

**Team
Acceptance**

**Action
Plan**

Clearly Defined Objectives

To set up your change for implementation, you need to have clearly defined objectives, team acceptance, and an action plan. These three elements form the sides of a powerful Change Management Triangle. We'll address developing clearly-defined objectives and gaining team acceptance in this chapter and crafting an action plan in Chapter 7: *Implementing Change.*

CLEARLY DEFINED OBJECTIVES

Establishing Base Camp

An ancient proverb says, "There are hundreds of paths up the mountain, all leading to the same place, so it doesn't matter which path you take. The only person wasting time is the one who runs around the mountain, telling others that their path is wrong."

All paths, though, start from a base camp. Once you have your mountaintop established, you need to figure out how far away that mountaintop is from your current position (base camp).

To figure out where to locate your base camp, especially if your mountaintop is far away, you must answer three specific questions.

Question 1: Why?

The response to "Why?" is often "Because"—and that's an awesome beginning. Humans will commit to a *because* since it gives them something to strive for and visualize. However, "because I told you" doesn't work with employees—at least not those that you want to stick around and support your change effort.

To communicate your *because* to your team, you must first clarify your *why* in your own mind.

Exercise: Clarifying Your "Why?"

What indicators, internally or externally, do you have that a change is required? (Use specific examples.)

_____

_____

_____

_____

How long have you been aware of these indicators and what have you attempted to change so far?

_____

_____

_____

Did those changes work? (Why/why not?)

_____

_____

_____

How has your business been or how will it be impacted because you haven't changed?

_____

_____

_____

How do you feel about that? (Frustrated, concerned, elated, content?)

_____

_____

_____

After going through this exercise do you still believe that your change is the right one? (Why/why not?)

_____

_____

_____

What will you do next?

_____

_____

_____

_____

Question 2: Why Now?

"Why now?" is a favorite question to ask clients when they seek coaching on a business decision. It's a very challenging question, especially for D- and I-style leaders whose typical response is, "Because I want to right now."

While it is true that rushing into a change effort can increase the risk of failure, delaying it may cause not only the change to fail but the organization as well.

Exercise: Clarifying Your "Why Now?"

Based on your answers from the previous exercises, why do you believe that you must implement your change now?

_____

_____

_____

_____

_____

_____

_____

Question 3: Why That?

"Why that?" as in "Why that particular change?" is the last crucial question to answer before establishing a base camp.

Exercise: Clarifying Your "Why That?"

What change do you plan to implement to resolve the challenges brought up in the previous exercises?

_____

_____

_____

_____

Why do you believe that change is the right one?

_____

_____

_____

_____

What alternatives did you consider before selecting that change?

_____

_____

_____

_____

Based on your "Why?," "Why now?," and "Why that?" answers, what is the *because* you will share with your team members to help them commit to supporting your change?

_____

_____

_____

_____

After you've established a base camp, next is, "What's the mountaintop?" or "Where do you want to be at the end of this change effort?" Whatever mountaintop you define is just the next peak in an ongoing series of mountaintops that stretch higher and higher.

Leaders frequently don't have an answer to that question. While the cliché about a journey of 1,000 miles beginning with a single step is true, few individuals would start a physical trip without a clear destination in mind. Without establishing a destination before starting, any destination will do. This is like someone setting a goal of earning "more" next year. By leaving "more" as the (vague) objective, this individual could earn $0.01 more than the previous year and still accomplish the goal.

THE PROBLEM WITH FAILURE

A reason most leaders don't have an answer to the "What's your mountaintop?" question isn't that they don't have a sense of where they want to end up or the positive benefits that will result. Rather, it's that they are afraid if they articulate the mountaintop, they might fail.

They come by this fear naturally. It was drilled into their heads by their parents and other authority figures when they were children. It lives in their Parent and Child ego state. This fear is especially prevalent in high achievers (in particular those who were successful at a young age) because the majority of the praise they received when they were younger was based on their successes.

To paraphrase David Sandler, when facing a decision imagine what the worst case scenario could be if you failed. If you can live with the worst case, act. If you can't, you have to decide if the price of inaction is too high. Put another way, ask yourself, "Is doing nothing an option given the worst case that could result?" If the answer is "yes," then don't do anything. If the answer is "no," as in "I must do something," then figure out what action you could take that might result in a worst case scenario with which you could live.

Exercise: Fear of Failure

What, specifically, makes you afraid to fail in this change effort?

_____

_____

_____

_____

If you were to fail, what is the worst that could happen?

_____

_____

_____

Can you live with the worst possible outcome? (yes/no): _____
If "yes," act!

If "no," consider either: 1) making yourself comfortable with the worst possible outcome or 2) modifying your proposed change so a different worst possible outcome could happen with which you would be comfortable.

_____

_____

_____

_____

The strength of any specific fear of failure is based on how you perceive yourself psychologically. Do you tend to see yourself as a winner or as a loser? Winners see themselves as winners psychologically, as part of their intrinsic identity, and not by their net worth, the title on their business card, or the number of people who buy tickets to see them perform. Winners understand that success means making choices. Choosing means one or both of a) potentially failing or b) saying "no" to another person.

Both of those outcomes, however, are things that people who don't instinctively identify as winners are trained to resist from childhood. For example, it's safer to say, "I will lose 4–6 pounds," instead of, "I will lose 5 pounds," because the latter goal is seen by non-winners as nothing but an opportunity to fail. The good news is: You can train yourself, over time, to see yourself as a winner. This takes time and effort, but it can (and must!) be done if behaviors are to change in a positive, sustainable way.

Bottom line: How you see yourself matters, and you must hold yourself accountable for the way you look at yourself. No thought lives rent-free in the human mind. It either supports a self-perception of "winner," or it doesn't.

This "winner" concept is encapsulated in Sandler's Identity/Role or I/R Theory. That theory states that our performance in our roles (the R-side) is directly related to how we see ourselves conceptually (the I-side). As David Sandler said, "You perform in your role in direct relation to how you see yourself conceptually."

As Sandler clients hear regularly, "You win, or you learn." If I only lose 4 pounds, that's still better than zero. I might have learned that I need to adjust my weight loss plan to lose 5 pounds.

Don't think because winners don't fear failure that they enjoy it. No one likes to fail. However, winners see failure as a growth opportunity instead of a definition of their self-worth.

Because humans are social animals, they are hardwired to say "yes" to other people. However, while saying "yes" might give a temporary dopamine rush, you might be pulled further away from your goals.

Winners apply a filter of, "Does [a choice or activity] advance me to my goals?" For example, if I have an endurance race tomorrow, and my friend whom I haven't seen in three years calls to invite me out for a drink (which will keep me out past the goal I set for going to bed), as a non-winner I think, "I'll just deal with being tired tomorrow." As a winner, I apply the "Does this advance me?" filter. I either suggest that we meet for a mid-afternoon coffee or invite my friend out after the race.

You might be thinking, "What happens if your friend is only in town for one night?" That's a fair question. Winners are also comfortable with risk. In this scenario, there's a risk that if my friend isn't available for coffee or is leaving early the following day, we might never see each other again. That's a low risk, but non-winners see every risk as colossal. This causes them to run around attempting to get their need for approval met at the expense of achieving their goals.

Winners understand that their brain is hardwired to prevent them from achieving their goals. Therefore, instead of setting wishy-washy goals like, "I'll exercise two to three times per week," they say, "I'll exercise two times per week," and give themselves permission to stretch to three times when two times becomes comfortable.

Non-winners can't articulate the path to their mountaintop. They say things like, "I'll figure it out." Winners don't "figure things out"; they have at least the skeleton of a plan to achieve a goal worked out before they start. Winners might set a goal of tripling their revenue in one year, but they will clearly understand what needs to be done by when to reach that goal.

Exercise: Figuring It Out

On a scale of 1–10, with 1 being "not at all" and 10 being "absolutely," do you have a mountaintop established for your change effort? _____

What is your mountaintop?

_____

_____

_____

_____

If you showed your score and your mountaintop to your most trusted advisor, what would he say (e.g., "You're too hard on yourself," "You're not hard enough," "Have you thought about...?")

_____

_____

_____

_____

What specific actions do you as leader need to take to raise that score or keep it at 10?

_____

_____

_____

_____

CHOOSING A LOWER PEAK

Armed with a clear understanding of where you are and where you want to be, you may feel that your base camp is too far from your mountaintop to be successful and that you need to choose a lower peak.

Choosing to lower your peak is OK, with the caveat that your original mountaintop must still be the ultimate goal. You chose that first mountaintop for a reason. Don't abandon it just because you feel slightly uncomfortable. As we'll discuss later, implementing and managing a change effort is a series of small mountaintops that rise to one giant peak.

Aiming at a lower peak can jump start your change because it is a change within a change. Just as Sandler's communications model is based on a series of small mutual agreements, your team members will be more OK with the transitions if you break the change into small parts. This leads to the second stage of Sandler's Change Management Triangle, Team Acceptance.

TEAM ACCEPTANCE

Accept that once you announce your change (or it gets announced for you), you have no control over the messaging—especially with team members who are well-versed in electronic communication. Remember that the first two stages of transition for each member of your team are denial and resistance. You can expect that some of your team members, especially the atheists, will talk to their colleagues, friends, and family about your change.

CASE IN POINT: LEVERAGING DISCONTENT IN A COMPETITOR'S SALES TEAM

The primary competitor of a communications company dramatically changed its compensation plan, which was posted about on public forums by several of the competitor's salespeople. The communications company used the discontent in its competitor's sales team to win several major accounts that were being underserviced by unhappy representatives.

You can, however, minimize the rumor mill by communicating clearly, confirming your team's understanding, and giving your team a *why*.

COMMUNICATING CLEARLY

One of the most important responsibilities of leaders—day-to-day and not just during change—is to create clarity between themselves and their teams. Creating clarity means avoiding buzzwords or euphemisms—e.g., "right-sizing," when you mean layoffs. As painful as clarity might be, you create greater pain and foment distrust when you use buzzwords or euphemisms.

Creating clarity also means taking into account the preferred communication style of each team member instead of communicating the way you like to give and receive information. If you are a C-style facts-and-detail person, remember to leave time for the people side of your change.

You must also consider the mode of communication you employ. In person, whether live or via a video conference, is always the best. In communication, a large part of the message comes from body language, a significant part from tonality, and just a small fraction comes from the actual words used.

When communicating voice-to-voice, tonality conveys almost the entire message because body language can't be seen. Text-based communication is best only for conveying information that has limited room for interpretation. Otherwise, your audience will decide your meaning and tone for you.

By communicating in plain language, using your body language, tonality, and words in concert with the style your audience prefers, you can greatly lower the chances of your change failing because of misinterpretation by your team.

CONFIRMING YOUR TEAM'S UNDERSTANDING

After closing a deal, especially one that was complex, a mentor of mine would say to his new client, "Thank you for your business. Would you tell me what you think you just bought?" I wish I could convey my mentor's very gentle way of asking that question. The new client's answer told him, while he was still right there, if he had any clarification to do before leaving. In this way, he avoided an awkward conversation with an unhappy client in the near future.

Some leaders have head trash (self-limiting beliefs and thought patterns) about asking a similar question because they find it condescending. This is probably because they had a condescending parent when they were children who asked them, "Do you understand me?" or "What did I just tell you?" in a critical tone. The fact is, everyone filters information differently. What leaders think they said and the message that gets interpreted can be dramatically different.

To give you a different example, I once spoke with a real estate agent about the area of the city in which her company specialized. Her response was "the inner city." However, after naming off a few neighborhoods that I considered "inner city," we discovered that our definitions were quite different.

Confirming your team's understanding reduces the potential for you to need to have an awkward conversation with them later when they aren't meeting your expectations. If they aren't, that is a failure on your part because your belief that they understood you caused you not to confirm that they understood.

CASE IN POINT: TOO MANY TOPICS, NOT ENOUGH INFORMATION

At the three-month review for one of my employees, her feedback under the question, "How can Hamish be a better leader?" read as follows: "Don't walk into my office to give me six ideas for things you want done and then just walk out."

This was a failure on my part as a leader. I wasn't confirming that she understood exactly what I expected before I left. We subsequently put two processes in place to ensure that both of us left each meeting with clarity as to what was expected by when.

First, we agreed that I would ask if she "had her notebook," which was code for, "I have information to share that you'll want to remember."

Second, we agreed that before I left her office, I would say, "Sorted?" (That's Scottish slang for "Everything in order?") If she replied, "Sorted," that meant she completely understood what I had asked her to do and the deadlines for completion. She also had permission to ask clarifying questions if she didn't understand the task or deadlines.

GIVING YOUR TEAM A "BECAUSE"

Humans are wired to seek meaning, then to act. When leaders fail to give the meaning behind the action they've asked their team to take, they create ambiguity. This ambiguity leads to anxiety, which leads to fear, which leads to paralysis and productivity loss.

Going back to the parenting example earlier, "because I said so" isn't going to create action in your team nor is it likely to generate much goodwill towards you. A *because* is personal to each of your team members just like their interpretation of your messaging is personal to each one. But even though each person on your team hears a different *because*, that doesn't mean they will be working counter to each other. Like the story of the three bricklayers, one who is "laying bricks," one who is "building a wall," and the other who is "building a cathedral," your team members can work toward the same mountaintop for different, personal reasons.

CASE IN POINT: BECAUSE OF...

Joel, the director of marketing, announced that the company was implementing a marketing automation program that would cause his team to be reduced by two people. One of those people, Brent, asked to meet with Joel.

BRENT: I appreciate you meeting with me about the new automation program, Joel.

JOEL: Absolutely, Brent. I'm curious why you wanted to talk.

BRENT: I'd like to lead the implementation.

JOEL: That's a very generous offer, Brent, especially as your position will be eliminated once the program is up and running. What's causing you to make this offer?

BRENT: Well, I was angry that I would be losing my job, but I figured that if I learn this system that is a skill I can transfer to another job. I'd prefer my last weeks with this company be positive for everyone.

JOEL: That's a great way of looking at your situation. The program does come with a consultant, who we already agreed to pay, but he will need a liaison internally. I'm OK with you being that person if you clearly document the processes you go through and train your colleagues who will be using the program before you go.

BRENT: That's fair, Joel.

JOEL: Glad to hear it. I'll expect a weekly progress meeting where you'll show me the documentation you've done so far. If I don't see that you're keeping your end of our deal, I'll pull you off the project. Are you OK with that?

> BRENT: Makes sense to me. How do I get connected with the consultant?
>
> JOEL: I'll introduce you by email this afternoon.

Joel could have stopped when he accepted Brent's offer; however, then there would have been no clarity around what he expected of Brent. By leveraging Brent's *because* (gaining a transferable skill), Joel created accountability for Brent with the consequence of being pulled off the project and not gaining that skill.

THIS CHAPTER IN 45 SECONDS

- There are no bad employees, only bad leaders.
- A successful change has clearly defined objectives, team acceptance, and an action plan.
- To establish clear objectives, you must first establish a base camp, which is where you are today.
- After establishing a base camp, you must define a mountaintop, or where you want to be after the change.
- Many leaders struggle with picking a mountaintop because they are afraid of failing.
- After you define your mountaintop, you may need to move your base camp.
- As it relates to your change, ask yourself, "Why?," "Why now?," and "Why that [change]?"
- Once you announce your change, you lose control of your messaging. You can minimize the rumor mill by communicating clearly, confirming understanding, and giving your team a *because*.

CHAPTER 6

What to Expect When You're Expecting Change

Leaders often forget that by the time they've created and implemented their plan, they have lived with the change longer than any member of their team. This gap causes them to lose perspective on the transitions that their team members need to experience.

As the old saying goes, "Inspect what you expect." Leaders who expect their team to immediately embrace change set themselves and their team members up for failure. These assumptions can be especially difficult for leaders who believe they have given their team the permission, protection, and potency required.

There are eight common consequences of transformative change, some or all of which will happen during your effort. Preparing yourself for these consequences will help you mitigate any potential damage you might cause by your expectations conflicting with reality.

CONSEQUENCE OF CHANGE #1: A SENSE OF LOSS

Think back to when you moved for the first time. Maybe you were a child, or maybe you didn't move until after you finished school. Either way, you probably felt some sense of loss. This feeling is the transition point between denial and exploration in transition. Leaders who aren't tuned into their team members' transition stages can push the team back into resistance by denying their need to grieve before moving forward.

CASE IN POINT: DENIAL TURNS INTO RESISTANCE

Tim and Dan's organization recently completed a move from a downtown office building to a corporate campus in the suburbs. Tim asked Dan for a meeting because he noticed Dan hadn't settled into their new offices yet, and he wanted to support Dan's transition (or at least, he thought he did).

TIM: Dan, may I ask you a direct question?

DAN: Um, sure, Tim. What's up?

TIM: Since we moved from downtown you've seemed out of sorts. I was curious what's going on and how I could support you as a leader.

DAN: Thanks for asking, Tim. You know, I haven't been comfortable since we moved. When we were downtown, I had my routines for getting in and going home each day, the baristas at the coffee shop next door knew my order...

TIM: Dan, sorry to cut you off. You're sad because your routine changed and you aren't a VIP at the local coffee shop?

DAN: Tim, that's not really fair.

TIM: What would be fair then? We moved six weeks ago! There are two coffee shops on campus, and we're closer to your house! When are you going to suck it up and get back to producing?

DAN: Tim, I'm done with this meeting. I feel like my feelings aren't being respected. I supported this move initially, but now I wonder if you and the company will support me.

TIM: Fine, Dan. We'll discuss this tomorrow morning.

Any loss, even if it is the loss of a favorite coffee shop, is personal. David Sandler's rule, "People buy emotionally and justify intellectually," also applies to change since your team members need to buy into it emotionally.

CASE IN POINT: DENIAL BECOMES EXPLORATION

Let's revisit Tim and Dan, with a different result.

TIM: Dan, may I ask you a direct question?

DAN: Um, sure, Tim. What's up?

TIM: Since we moved from downtown you've seemed out of sorts. I was curious what's going on and how I could support you as leader.

DAN: Thanks for asking, Tim. You know, I haven't been comfortable since we moved. When we were downtown, I had my routines for getting in and going home each day, the baristas at the coffee shop next door knew my order, and I knew where everything was around us. For the past six weeks, I've felt like something's missing.

TIM: Oh. What do you feel that is?

DAN: My wife asked me the same question last night. After we had talked about it a bit, I came to the conclusion that it was the sense of security that came with all of those things I just mentioned.

TIM: And?

DAN: And I know that what I had downtown is gone, and I need to move forward so I can build up that sense of security here.

TIM: How can I support you in that?

DAN: Frankly, I don't know that you can. But I would appreciate it if you see me moping around give me a little shake and get me moving.

TIM: HR might have an issue with me giving you a little shake.

DAN (smiling): Probably not physically. But you're welcome to say, "You seem a little off today."

TIM: I can do that. Thanks for chatting.

DAN: You're welcome. Appreciate you kicking me out of my funk.

CONSEQUENCE OF CHANGE #2: CONFUSION AND AMBIVALENCE

Despite the best effort on your part, your team may still experience confusion and ambivalence about your change. When they do, your comfort level with being vulnerable—the position of greatest strength for a leader—will determine how well you mitigate this consequence.

Being vulnerable in this case means taking the responsibility for causing confusion among your team members and exploring their confusion instead of reacting to it.

CASE IN POINT: VULNERABILITY SAVES THE CHANGE

Toni and her team restructured their account management process last month. Any account that hadn't purchased in the previous six months was transferred to their inside sales team unless there was an active opportunity that was expected to close in the next 30 days in their CRM.

One of Toni's veteran salespeople Jessica stopped Toni in the hallway and confronted her about this change.

JESSICA: Toni, I'm totally lost on this account management process.

TONI: Thanks for saying so, Jessica. What's causing you to be lost?

JESSICA: Well, I don't get the timelines at all. The way I heard it, I lose every account that hasn't bought from me in six months.

TONI: Ah, I get it. That's my fault, Jessica. Yes, any account that hasn't purchased from you in the last six months will transfer to Inside Sales unless you happen to have an active opportunity that will close in the next 30 days in the CRM.

JESSICA: Yeah, still don't get it.

TONI: Let me put it another way. XYZ Inc. is one of your accounts, right?

JESSICA: Right, but they're regular buyers.

TONI: That's OK. Let's pretend they aren't.

JESSICA: All right.

TONI: So, XYZ Inc. hasn't bought anything from you since January, and let's say that it's June. When do they transfer to Inside Sales?

JESSICA: I guess at the end of the month.

TONI: Right. Unless you happen to re-engage XYZ in June and open up a new opportunity that will close in the next 30 days.

JESSICA: So, if I opened up an opportunity on June 7, I'd have until July 7 to close it?

TONI: Exactly. How fuzzy is the account management picture now?

JESSICA: Now it's clear. Thank you for explaining.

TONI: You're welcome.

By accepting responsibility for causing Jessica's confusion, Toni gave Jessica the opportunity to explore her confusion, and then move forward.

CONSEQUENCE OF CHANGE #3: REDUCED TRUST

Trust is built through consistency. In change, little is consistent. Like the trust that the floor will remain stable erodes during an earthquake, trust between you and your team will erode during the change. This consequence is especially difficult for I- and S-style leaders to manage because of their people orientation.

To overcome reduced trust between you and your team members, find ways to create consistency. It could be something small, like having a daily six-minute stand-up meeting with your team to specifically discuss victories, impending events, and problems related to your change (in my training, we call this a "VIP session"). Everyone must bring a V, I, or P to share. V's are celebrated. I's are clarified (e.g., "When you say, 'The client feedback form will be functional by tomorrow,' what do you mean by 'functional'?"). P's are either quickly solved by your team, or specific action items are agreed upon to eliminate that problem.

Exercise: Creating Consistency

What could you do to create consistency during your change effort? Be as specific as possible (e.g., if you plan to have a daily VIP session, when would it happen, who would be involved, and how would you celebrate V's, clarify I's and eliminate P's?).

_____

_____

_____

_____

CONSEQUENCE OF CHANGE #4: INCREASED CONCERNS ABOUT SURVIVAL

You probably have at least one person on your team who has experienced, or had someone close to him experience, losing a job as part of a change. Depending on how vocal that person is, this consequence could be a major headache for you.

When your change is implemented, your team will seek reassurance that they will be OK, especially as it relates to job security. Until your team members feel reassured, they will stay in the resistance stage of transition.

Granted, sometimes leaders can't provide total reassurance, especially during a merger/acquisition, industry fluctuations, or a severe economic decline. What leaders can do in that case is provide as much reassurance as they can, or are allowed to, while providing clarity as to when they will update their team again.

CASE IN POINT: REASSURING IN SMALL BITES

Because of a sudden and severe reduction in commodity prices, rumors started in Sheila's company that layoffs would happen shortly. Abby, one of Sheila's newer team members, approached her about layoffs.

ABBY: Sheila, will there be layoffs?

SHEILA: Thanks for asking, Abby. What are you hoping I'll say?

ABBY: Well, "no" would be great.

SHEILA: I'd love to do that, Abby. The fact is I'm working

with the other members of the executive team on some different scenarios to keep the company afloat until commodity prices recover.

ABBY: That doesn't really help, Sheila.

SHEILA: Fair enough, Abby. May I share a couple of thoughts with you?

ABBY: OK. What?

SHEILA: Number one, each of us can choose to have either an outlook of possibility or limitation. In these times, it's easy to have an outlook of limitation because people are losing their jobs and companies are going under. But we have to remember that what we're experiencing right now is part of the cycle. We can choose to hide under our desks and hope things get better, or we can be proactive and take control of our destiny. Which sounds better to you?

ABBY: The first one sounds easier, but the second one sounds better.

SHEILA: Glad to have you on the outlook of possibility team, Abby. Second, I saw someone from Sandler speak at a conference once. One of the things he said that stuck with me was, "Never manage anything you can't control." What does that mean to you?

ABBY: Maybe, "Don't worry about losing my job because I can't control that"?

SHEILA: That's a good start. What can you control?

ABBY: How I do my job, I guess.

SHEILA: That's true, Abby. Here's what I know about companies going through one of these cycles—they still want to keep good people on their teams. It may mean those people have to take pay cuts to stay, but they get to keep their job.

ABBY: So what you're saying is if I perform well, I'll probably keep my job?

SHEILA: I wish it could be that black and white, Abby. Layoffs are a last resort for us, but they may happen. The last to go would be the people who continue to move the organization forward despite forces beyond their control.

ABBY: That wasn't totally what I hoped for, but I see that you probably couldn't give me more than what you did. Thanks, Sheila.

SHEILA: You're welcome, Abby. I'm glad you asked.

CONSEQUENCE OF CHANGE #5: COMMUNICATION PROBLEMS

Each member of your team will feel overwhelmed at some point during the transition. As a team leader, you are responsible for guiding everyone through that period of overwhelm by actively listening and responding appropriately.

A Word on Active Listening

People who are "actively listening" give feedback to their conversation partners through paraphrasing or restating what their partner said.

Paraphrasing would sound like:

DOUG: How's the new product launch going, Susan?

SUSAN: Great! We've launched in California, Oregon, and

Washington and plan to launch in Arizona next week.

DOUG: Glad to hear we've got the West Coast covered.

Restatement would sound like:

DOUG: How's the new product launch going, Susan?

SUSAN: Great! We've launched in California, Oregon, and Washington and plan to launch in Arizona next week.

DOUG: Glad to hear we've launched in California, Oregon, and Washington and Arizona is launching next week.

While paraphrasing is useful for summarizing, restatement is the best active listening technique for difficult conversations. When people are emotionally engaged in a conversation, sometimes they say things that are a reaction to the situation instead of a measured response. By using restatement, you give the other speaker an opportunity to hear his words again and, potentially, prevent an emotional conversation from escalating into a conflict.

Some leaders spend hours of their own and their team's time crafting PowerPoints and FAQ documents in the belief that those intellectual devices will convince the team to support the change. These tools have their place (the C-style members of your team will appreciate them), but communication is a two-way activity that starts with you, the leader, actively listening to the concerns of your team.

Because communication problems, especially during change, are usually the cause or result of conflict, your best active listening technique is restatement instead of paraphrasing. In paraphrasing, you use your words to send back what you heard your team members say, which can cause conflict to escalate because they may feel you didn't understand them. By restating verbatim, you say back the exact words your team members said. This restatement leverages a saying of David Sandler's: "They can't argue with their own data." Restatement creates clarity between two people and allows the brain's cognitive functions to take over from the primal, emotional areas.

CASE IN POINT: PARAPHRASING VS. RESTATEMENT

Dionne and Fred were peers in the marketing department transitioning to using a digital workflow system to manage projects. Dionne was an advocate of the workflow system while Fred had been largely agnostic. Fred approached Dionne for support on correcting a data-entry error that made it appear a project on which he was still working was completed.

Paraphrasing

FRED: Dionne, is there anyone in this building who can tell me what I need to do to get this idiotic system to let me re-open this project?

DIONNE: I can help you with that, Fred. Sounds frustrating.

FRED:. I'm afraid this stupid system will give me a heart attack before the day's out.

DIONNE: So you're frustrated with the workflow system, and you're worried about the impact on your work. I get it.

FRED: I'm not "worried about the impact on my work," Dionne. Forget it. I'll figure it out later.

FRED leaves.

Restatement

FRED: Dionne, is there anyone in this building who can tell me what I need to do to get this idiotic system to let me re-open this project?

DIONNE: I can help you with that, Fred. Sounds frustrating.

FRED: I'm afraid this stupid system will give me a heart attack before the day's out.

DIONNE: How's the system going to give you a heart attack before the day is out?

FRED: Well... That is... OK, I am frustrated, Dionne. Mostly at myself. I tried to save myself a bit of time doing data entry, made a mistake, and I'm worried that Alisha will think that the project is done and add more to my plate.

DIONNE: Makes sense, Fred. How about we get that project undone right now so you can keep working on it until it's really finished?

FRED: That would be great. Thanks, Dionne.

Even though saying back something like "give you a heart attack" may sound silly to you, to the people who might have just said those words, they have real, emotional meaning. Helping them hear themselves gives them a chance to de-escalate on their own.

CONSEQUENCE OF CHANGE #6: LOWER PRODUCTIVITY

During a change, productivity often suffers. As a leader, you'll want to base your productivity expectations on what will result once the change has been fully implemented, not what happens at every step of the way. Try not to be too attached to the short-term processes; focus instead on the long-term outcomes.

If your implementation plan includes a strong accountability structure for not only your change process but also day-to-day business as you transition, then this consequence will be largely mitigated.

Even with a good accountability structure in place, however, productivity will dip as team members go through their personal transitions. This is not a time for you to accept lower productivity or invite it by saying things like, "I know you have a lot on your plate right now, so it's OK for your output to be lower." Instead, incentivize your team to continue producing at or above their current rate, especially when it comes to activities that support the change effort.

Incentives are usually either time or money based. The most motivating incentives are ones that tie directly to supporting an individual team member's personal goals.

CASE IN POINT: INCENTIVES TIED TO SUPPORTING CHANGE

The partners of a small consulting company were tired of chasing bad leads that came in from their website. One of the partners knew that their marketer had a goal of purchasing her first house within the year and had been saving for some time for a down payment. As part of a website redesign project she had already started, the partners presented her with an incentive plan that paid her a bonus for every qualified lead that came in through the website. To be qualified, the lead had to meet specific criteria. Five months after being presented with the incentive plan, their marketer had enough saved for a down payment.

Incentives need not be large (e.g., $1,000 for every qualified lead in the Case in Point above), but they need to be big enough to prompt action in that individual (e.g., $1 for every qualified lead isn't an incentive to change).

When trust is temporarily reduced and confusion exists, incentives must be easy to both understand and achieve by all members of the group. To be effective, your incentives should pass the "if you do this, you get that" test. Similar to animals who learn that if they push a specific lever then they get a treat, your team should be able to understand clearly what behavior is rewarded and the type of reward they would receive. While you may find the analogy of your team as a group of animals in a lab unsettling, humans are animals and leadership is a science. During the change, your team members have enough on their minds without also having to figure out a complicated new incentive plan.

Exercise: Your Incentives

What behavior will you incentivize during your change effort? This could be change-specific or day-to-day behavior you want to keep at or above current performance.

_____

_____

_____

_____

What incentives (time or money) will you offer for the behavior(s)?

_____

_____

_____

_____

If you were a team member learning about those incentives, why would they motivate you?

_____

_____

_____

_____

CONSEQUENCE OF CHANGE #7: TURNOVER

Earlier in this book we talked about the bottom 20% of your organization, the atheists, who will resist change until they either defeat it, grudgingly accept it, or leave the organization. More often than not, they choose to "be successful elsewhere."

What's troubling is the number of leaders who are totally shocked by turnover even when an employee effectively says, "If you do this, I'll quit."

Because managed turnover is part of any professionally led organization, a plan to replace people who self-select or are terminated as part of the change is likely in place already. However, the volume of people needing to be replaced simultaneously as well as the steep learning curve new employees have to traverse to become productive members of the team means that using an organization's standard onboarding plan is likely to cause frustration for both the employees and the leader.

To effectively onboard during a change, focus less on the behaviors an employee needs to do to become a valuable, long-term member of your team and instead focus on creating a minimally valuable employee (MVE).

MVEs are very valuable in a specific area. They may initially start as consultants who bring a few very specific skills to your team but have either the cognitive abilities to add new skills or already possess others that are underdeveloped. For example, you may hire a communications professional well-versed in internal communications whom you leverage to communicate to the organization. An onboarding plan for an MVE would include three to five specific, measurable behaviors that, if executed, would support the change and enable you to test if the new employee could become a valuable, long-term contributor. The timeframe for this onboarding plan could be 30 days, which is plenty of time for you to observe your new hire and determine if you want to keep him.

Exercise: Your MVE Onboarding Plan

Looking at your implementation plan, what role do you believe you will most likely need to replace or add support for during your change effort?

_____

_____

_____

_____

What specific one or two skill sets would an MVE bring to your team?

_____

_____

_____

_____

What three to five specific, measurable behaviors would you ask your MVEs to execute to 1) support your change effort and 2) demonstrate that they could be valuable, long-term contributors?

_____

_____

_____

_____

_____

_____

_____

_____

CONSEQUENCE OF CHANGE #8: EXPRESSION OF STRONG FEELINGS

The consequence of a change in which team members express strong feelings typically troubles D- and C-style leaders. They tend to say, or at least think, things like, "Suck it up and do as I say," or "Here are the 17 intellectual reasons why this makes sense for you and the organization." By now you probably appreciate that most of your team members don't process information the way you do. Instead of resisting their need to vent, welcome it while keeping them accountable for supporting your change effort.

When team members are expressing their feelings, don't give them a lot of information or instructions. The human brain's emotional processing unit gets overloaded easily, which may push your team members into the resistance stage of transition. Feed them small bites of information until their cognitive functions re-assert themselves.

CASE IN POINT: LET THEM VENT, BUT NOT TOO LONG

Bryan's team member Jonathan seemed agitated in their group meeting to discuss progress on changing over to an enterprise resource management software program that would unite four separate software programs. Bryan asked Jonathan to stay after the rest of their team dispersed.

BRYAN: Jonathan, my sense is you're uncomfortable with something we discussed this morning. Is that fair?

JONATHAN: Yeah, it is.

BRYAN: What is it?

JONATHAN: It's like we're talking in circles! Every day we stand up and talk about what's happening next, and the answer is nothing. If we're going to implement this ERM program, let's get it done so we can move on with our jobs.

BRYAN: That's fair, Jonathan. I'm curious. When you say that every day nothing is happening, what do you mean?

JONATHAN: That the pace of this implementation is making me tired. I can't see it ever ending.

BRYAN: I appreciate you telling me that, Jonathan. What can we do to make you feel like there's an ending in sight?

JONATHAN: I'm not sure.

BRYAN: Have you ever climbed a mountain, Jonathan?

JONATHAN: No, why do you ask?

BRYAN: A friend of mine once climbed a mountain with a group of other executives. None of them had any previous mountaineering experience. During their orientation, their guide told them that if they kept looking at the top of the mountain while they were climbing, they would get discouraged because it would seem like they weren't making progress. Instead, they should focus on the next three steps they had to take, especially because at some points the terrain was quite dangerous, and only occasionally look at the top. If they did that, they would stay motivated.

JONATHAN: So if I focus on what I need to do to today to have something to report tomorrow, then I might not feel so annoyed at how long this implementation is taking?

BRYAN: Probably. How about we test that out over the next week and discuss it again?

JONATHAN: Sounds good to me, Bryan. I have a few things to get to before tomorrow's meeting.

By staying emotionally unattached and being curious about the source of Jonathan's frustration, Bryan was able to steer him back to taking action in support of their change effort instead of wallowing in his emotions.

THIS CHAPTER IN 45 SECONDS

- There are eight consequences of change, some or all of which will happen with your team members:
  - ◊ Sense of loss
  - ◊ Confusion and ambivalence
  - ◊ Reduced trust
  - ◊ Increased concerns about survival
  - ◊ Communication problems
  - ◊ Lower productivity
  - ◊ Turnover
  - ◊ Feelings
- Just as prospects buy emotionally and justify their decision intellectually, your team members are buying into your change emotionally.
- Allow them to experience their sense of loss as a way to move them to the exploration stage of transition.
- As a leader, you must take responsibility for eliminating ambiguity on your team.

- Trust is created through consistency. Create a small measure of consistency, like a daily VIP session, to at least maintain trust during the change.
- Never try to manage anything you can't control.
- Use restatement instead of paraphrasing to stop communication problems from escalating.
- Incentives, especially those that relate to activities supporting your change, can keep productivity up as your team transitions.
- Incentives must pass the "if I do this, then I get that" test, or they will be detrimental to your change effort.
- When onboarding new team members during the change, focus on creating minimally valuable employees over their first 30 days through three to five specific, measurable behaviors that support your change effort.
- Should employees successfully execute those behaviors, they may become long-term members of your team.
- Allow your team members to vent, but keep them accountable for executing the activities they need to do to support your change and continue day-to-day business.

CHAPTER 7

Implementing Change

N ow that you've established a base camp and your ultimate
mountaintop and achieved team acceptance, you're ready to
implement. It's time to talk about creating a change implementation plan.

While it might sound contrary to implementation, Sandler
considers creating an action plan to be part of the implementation
stage because by collaborating with your team to create the plan
you leverage your angels and convert the agnostics.

When implementing change, especially as you create your
roadmap, you must remember that you can't a) predict or b) control
everything that will happen. Leaders typically fall into two camps
when they hear that. Either they decide they shouldn't bother
with planning at all, which is an obvious mistake, or they try to
plan and plan and plan and plan and plan until they feel they have

accounted for every possible variable. Those in the latter group will discover that their opportunity to implement change has passed, potentially putting their organization in a disadvantaged position.

THE RACI MODEL FOR IMPLEMENTING CHANGE

A simple model many organizations use to implement change successfully is RACI, or assigning people to the roles of responsible, accountable, consulted, and informed.

Responsible	Accountable	Consulted	Informed

At any point in the change, you, the leader, are the one sitting in the "A" box. You are **accountable** for the success or failure of this change effort. If that idea makes you uncomfortable, then you aren't the right individual to lead the change. Anyone in a leadership role in your organization is also accountable. While one of your direct reports might be in the "responsible" box in your RACI chart, they will be in the "accountable" box in their own RACI chart.

Responsible individuals are those actively involved in implementing and managing the change. The list of responsible individuals will extend from direct reports down to the front lines of the organization.

Individuals who are **consulted** are involved in the planning, implementation, and management stages as resources because they possess expertise or have the power to stop or continue a change effort. These individuals could be members of your board or trusted advisors whom you rely on for guidance. They could also be selected members of your team who could be angels. By consulting these potential angels before implementation, you increase their commitment because your change becomes their change.

CASE IN POINT: FAILING TO CONSULT AN AFFECTED GROUP

The CFO of a client in the telecommunications industry was frustrated with the number of clients who paid their invoices past 30 days. After discussing this with his leadership team, he instructed his accounts receivable group to send a letter to all of their clients who had consistently (more than twice in a quarter) paid their invoices past 30 days. This letter stated that future late payments would result in revocation of that client's net-30 credit status and placement on payment up front.

The CFO forgot to inform his sales team that these letters would be sent, so the representatives didn't have the chance to prepare clients for the new terms. This new policy caused the company to lose an account worth 14% of annual revenue that had been allowed net-45 payment terms.

Subsequently, this company moved all of its clients to net-30 and trained the sales team to bring up payment terms in their qualifying steps to reduce time wasted with prospects who wouldn't agree to net-30.

Someone who is **informed** doesn't have any involvement other than receiving information about your change effort and its progress. These individuals may be outside your organization and include strategic partners, clients, or vendors. They could also be members of your team who need more time to accept that a change will happen. They could become strong atheists if it happens too quickly (in their opinion).

Exercise: Who Is RACI in Your Change?

In the chart below, list the individuals who will be responsible, consulted, and informed of your change. Your name goes in the "accountable" box.

Responsible	Accountable	Consulted	Informed

A common mistake that leaders, including myself, make when using RACI is writing down the name of a department or group instead of an individual. Yes, Shipping/Receiving may be responsible for implementing your new just-in-time delivery process, but to successfully move your team into the exploration and commitment stages of transition, you must create complete clarity around the *who*, *what*, *when*, *where*, *why*, and *how*, of your change effort. This clarity starts with naming specific individuals in your RACI chart. Just because someone is named in one box today doesn't mean he would remain in that box or on your chart at all tomorrow. A change plan, of which RACI is a small part, isn't a carved block of granite with specific instructions that will guarantee success. It's more like the basic structure of a sonnet, which provides specific requirements while still giving the poet infinite ways to create and express an idea.

CASE IN POINT: CHANGING COMPENSATION PLAN FOR SALES TEAM

A communication services company shifted its compensation model from quarterly commission payouts to an annual commission payout, but still kept quarterly sales targets for its team. Missing a quarterly target created a significant penalty on a salesperson's annual commission check. Motivation plummeted because salespeople who didn't hit their quarterly target in Q1 or Q2 had zero incentive to sell in Q3 and Q4 because they had already accrued a significant financial penalty with no apparent way to minimize or cancel that penalty.

The following year, management collaboratively built a compensation structure with its sales team that returned to quarterly commission payouts. Motivation improved, and sales in Q3 and Q4 of the following year were significantly higher than the year before.

COLLABORATIVELY CREATING A ROADMAP FOR CHANGE

Leaders who fear the concept of collaboration should stop reading and start figuring out how they will explain why their change effort failed.

Many current leaders-in-training, most of which come from the Millennial generation, have been practicing collaboration their entire lives and are confused when their leaders don't want to collaborate with them.

Collaboration isn't giving up control. In fact, just as the lead dog in a bobsled sets the pace, when it comes to accountability so too does the leader set the pace for planning.

What has been successful is leaders defining the mountaintop and base camp, soliciting feedback from their teams to confirm that everyone is on the same page, and then guiding their teams backwards from the mountaintop to create an implementation plan.

CASE IN POINT: CREATING A CHANGE PLAN WITH A PROSPECT

Cynthia sold industrial safety management systems for remote plants. She met with Donald, the vice president of safety. Donald oversaw a network of 18 remote plants. He was under pressure to get a safety management system in place before the end of the calendar year or risk losing the company's operating license from the territory's legislature.

CYNTHIA: Donald, may I use your whiteboard?

DONALD: Sure, go ahead.

Cynthia draws a long horizontal line bookended by two short vertical lines.

CYNTHIA: Donald, today is what?

DONALD: April 7.

Cynthia writes "April 7" under the short line to the left.

CYNTHIA: Great. Let's pretend that everything works out between us and we choose to work together. When would you need a safety management system up and running?

DONALD: November 30.

Cynthia writes "November 30" under the short line to the right.

CYNTHIA: Thank you. Is it November 30 for a reason?

DONALD: Yes. We need to have our certification completed by December 31. It typically takes at least one week to get inspectors out to our sites and another week to get their approval.

CYNTHIA: Thanks for helping me understand. What happens if we don't hit November 30?

DONALD: We'll probably lose our license to operate until we get our certification in, which likely means the end of January with the last half of December being a wash.

CYNTHIA: Wow. That's a lot of pressure on you.

DONALD: Don't I know it.

CYNTHIA: Donald, there are two sides to this interaction, "you" and "me"—not in an adversarial way, but there's your side of the table and mine. Is that fair?

DONALD: That's fair.

Cynthia writes "you" above the long horizontal line and "me" below it.

CYNTHIA: So Donald, working back from November 30, would you walk me through the boxes you need to check internally to get a safety system, mine or anyone else's, up and running by November 30?

DONALD: Well, first we'd need to...

Donald shares the steps and people involved as Cynthia notes them on the board.

CYNTHIA: Thank you, Donald. There are some boxes I'd need to check on my side, too. May I share them with you?

DONALD: Absolutely.

By clearly laying out the next steps and deadlines required to meet an implementation deadline and the consequences for not hitting it, Cynthia and Donald collaboratively build a plan that will guide their work together. The same principle can be adopted to change planning.

CASE IN POINT: CHANGE TIMELINE

Brad meets with his team members Joanne, Tim, Deborah, and Mike to map out an impending office move. When his team enters their conference room, Brad has a long horizontal line and two small vertical lines drawn on their whiteboard.

BRAD: Our new office is confirmed ready for September 25.

Brad writes "September 25" under the right vertical line.

BRAD: We must be completely out of this space by

September 29, or our landlord will penalize us. The purpose of this meeting is to figure out how we get from today, August 2...

Brad writes "August 2" under the left vertical line.

BRAD: ...to being completely out by September 29.

JOANNE: Are we setting ourselves up to fail by shooting for September 25? What if we're ready, and our new office isn't?

BRAD: Good point, Joanne. I spoke with our contractors, and they assured me that we could move in on the 22nd. They wanted to give themselves a couple of days of wiggle room just in case. Does that help?

JOANNE: Yes, thank you.

BRAD: Is everyone comfortable with September 25 as move-in date?

The group nods.

BRAD: Great. In that case, let's work backwards to today to figure out how we get to there from here.

Brad makes notes on the board from the following discussion.

MIKE: We'll need phone and internet hooked up and ready, so we don't have much downtime.

BRAD: Good. When should that be done?

MIKE: They could do it the morning of the 25th, but the 22nd would be better.

BRAD: OK, let's do the 22nd then.

JOANNE: We'll need to notify our vendors and clients of our new address by the first of September.

BRAD: Good point, Joanne. Are you OK to be accountable for that getting done?

JOANNE: Sure, I'll talk to Accounting about sending out a message in August.

TIM: The movers will need to be scheduled this week.

BRAD: Tim, would you take that on? By when should we expect that done?

TIM: I'll reach out for quotes today and have a decision by the end of Thursday.

BRAD: Thank you.

DEBORAH: What about packing? We've got a lot of equipment, furniture, and supplies. Are you expecting us to pack up all of it?

BRAD: Good question, Deborah. I hadn't thought of that. What do all of you think?

TIM: I know some movers who will pack, too. Let me add that to my quote request.

BRAD: Thanks, Tim. What else haven't we talked about?

DEBORAH: That looks like the big stuff.

The group nods.

BRAD: Great. I'll take a picture of this and email it to you, so all of us are on the same page. I'll print a copy, too, and post in here so we can check our accountabilities off.

Because change is conceptual, using a timeline and co-creating steps back from your mountaintop to base camp makes it concrete and easier for your team members to accept. This process helps springboard them through resistance and denial into the exploration phase of their transition.

MANAGING AMBIGUITY, ANXIETY, AND FEAR IN CHANGE

A major consequence of change, to be explored in Chapter 8, is that it creates ambiguity in your team members' world.

Ambiguity on its own isn't a major issue—humans can handle ambiguity for a time. Think of friends who ask to meet you at a local coffee shop "at 2:00 P.M." If you show up at 2:00 P.M. and they aren't there, you'll likely think something like, "Maybe they said, 'Around 2:00,' so I'll wait a few minutes."

The longer ambiguity exists, the more likely it is to turn into anxiety. Anxiety is a constant low-level stress that eats away at people's mental and emotional energy reserves, prompting them to focus on their anxiety instead of what they wanted to accomplish. Going back to the coffee shop example, if it's now 2:15 P.M. and your friends haven't arrived, you'll likely think something like, "Maybe they said a different coffee shop. Maybe they said tomorrow, not today. I'll text them."

Fear is an amplification of anxiety, increasing stress on a person's mental and emotional energy reserves. Because human brains are wired to imagine worst case scenarios as a survival mechanism, once anxiety turns to fear, people tend to become paralyzed. They focus only on the worst case scenario and those that will come after. Returning to the coffee shop example: If it's now 2:25 P.M. with no response to your texts or calls, you might think something like, "Maybe they were in an accident. Maybe they're in the hospital—or dead!"

You cannot avoid creating ambiguity during your change effort. However, you can limit ambiguity, reduce anxiety, and (mostly) eliminate fear by asking yourself if you are providing a safe COVE (clear, open, vulnerable, expectations) for your team members to shelter in while they transition. COVE is also a checklist for guiding yourself or your team through change successfully.

Clear

Have you been clear about the reasons for the change? Could your team answer, "Why?," "Why now?," and "Why that [change]?" as they relate to it? Could you? If not, you might have created ambiguity, which could soon turn to anxiety and fear.

CASE IN POINT: LACK OF CLARITY CAUSES FEAR RESISTANCE

Steve was frustrated with his direct report Don, who was supposed to use their team's intranet-based calendar for marking any absences from the office. However, Don was only using the calendar to mark his vacations and continued to use their team's shared spreadsheet for any other absences, such as trade shows or site visits.

STEVE: Don, I'm confused. We implemented the intranet calendar system six weeks ago and all you've got in there is your vacation. I know you have site visits planned, and we had that situation last week where we had to call you while you were out because we needed some information from you right away and thought you were in the office.

DON: I'm confused too, Steve. My understanding is the intranet calendar was just for vacations because HR has access to that, but we'd continue to use the spreadsheet if we were out of the office for any other reason.

STEVE: Oh. How did you get that impression?

DON: Well, when you told us about the intranet calendar what I heard was, "HR requires that we use this to track vacations."

STEVE: Ah. My fault, Don. I didn't make sure that everyone on the team, including you, understood that we were switching to the intranet calendar because HR required it, but that we would post all of our absences there to avoid having multiple calendars to check.

DON: I probably should have listened past, "HR requires." Thanks for clearing that up. I'll make sure that all scheduled out-of-office days are in the intranet calendar by tomorrow.

STEVE: Thanks, Don. Let me know how I can support you with that.

By asking a question to test Don's understanding of the change instead of playing "gotcha," Steve learned that Don's failure to use the calendar properly lay with him. He now also knew that he likely created mystification with more members of his team than just Don.

Open

Has your communication about the change been open and effective? Each member of your team gives and receives information differently and their focus, present or future, could be different from yours. If your team can't answer "why?," "why now?," and "why that [change]?" as it relates to your new initiative, then your communication may not have been open or effective. One challenge leaders have with open communication is that some changes, like mergers and acquisitions, require some level of secrecy from a legal perspective. What they forget is humans abhor ambiguity because it turns into anxiety, which can become fear. They will then fill the vacuum of ambiguity with their own stories. Research exists that shows humans will accept a response that is less than what they asked for if the response comes with a *because*.

CASE IN POINT: YOU'LL KNOW WHEN I CAN TELL YOU

A technology company was near the closing of a round of financing when a rumor started among the staff that the financing was really an acquisition of the company's intellectual property that, once completed, would mean the loss of their jobs. The CEO stumbled across this rumor when one of his friends congratulated him on his "exit."

After checking with a couple of the senior team members, the CEO called an all-hands meeting and laid bare everything he was legally allowed to tell them, which included a strong message that their jobs were secure, and the company was in a sound financial position. The CEO concluded his remarks with, "I can't share the details with you now because we're still negotiating, but we will share them with you when we are legally allowed."

The CEO still lost a few members of the team who were frustrated that the boss wouldn't share everything with them, but the rest were content with the *because* that their CEO had shared with them.

Vulnerable

Are you being vulnerable when communicating? Are you good at acknowledging to others that you have both strengths and weaknesses, that you have made your share of mistakes in life, that you need help from other people in those areas where you don't know the best way forward? Vulnerability creates strength and credibility in a leader. Even in very hierarchical organizations, an "I don't know, but we'll figure it out" from a leader carries more weight than pretending to have everything squared away, all the time. (By the way, there are leaders who attempt to figure everything out before implementing change, but because they waste so much time planning, their ideas become irrelevant by the time change is upon them.)

Exercise: Vulnerability

What concerns you about being vulnerable in your communications with your team?

_____

_____

_____

_____

What are the consequences of coming across to others as someone who claims to have no weaknesses or vulnerabilities?

_____

_____

_____

_____

Expectations

Are you managing expectations? "We're launching a new benefits program" means something different to each person who hears that message, both regarding content (what the program will contain) and timing (when the program will be implemented). Part of the clarity you must create is in setting and managing expectations. For example, if your change is to have everyone stop checking their phones when in meetings, manage expectations with your team that show you understand the "phones in meetings" switch can't just be flicked to the "off" position. Human beings are fallible. Your change will result in failures, but those failures don't mean that it won't be successful overall.

In managing expectations, especially during personal changes, it will be beneficial to have someone challenge you if yours drifts into setting yourself up for failure. Being clear about the reasons for change with yourself and your team, openly and effectively communicating the reasons and the path you'll follow up front, while being vulnerable and managing expectations, significantly reduce or eliminate the ambiguity, anxiety, and fear inherent when change happens.

*Exercise: Eliminating Ambiguity, Anxiety
and Fear in Your Change*

What specific actions will you take to eliminate ambiguity, anxiety, and fear in your team during your change?

_____

_____

_____

_____

SET EXPECTATIONS AND ACCOUNTABILITIES

It is critical to impress on every member of your team that your change effort and their transitions won't be one straight shot to the top of a single mountain, but instead a series of small summits leading to the destination peak. These smaller summits will become your new base camp after successful transitions and changes are complete for that phase. Put another way: Your new base camp will be the result of a successful change, not part of one. Skipping this step will cause you to waste time with team members who are feeling uncomfortable with the pace of your implementation, whether it is (to them) slow or fast.

Circling back to DISC for a moment, the D- and I-style members of your team may feel that you are moving too slow because they believe the small summits you and your team created are too easy to reach (the D-styles) or that your slow pace is making implementation boring (the I-styles). The S- and C-style team members may feel that you are moving too fast because they and their colleagues are feeling uncomfortable (the S-styles) or that your pace is prompting some members of the team to take shortcuts that don't follow your implementation plan (the C-styles). We'll address how to handle those conversations in Chapter 8: *Managing Change.*

Speaking of different DISC styles and a series of small summits, your implementation plan will likely have different members of your team acting as the sherpa for a specific summit. However, you are the ultimate sherpa because you will be guiding your team through their transitions as well. Selecting a sherpa to reach one of your small summits benefits your change effort in two ways. First, you enroll that team member in becoming an angel, at least for that stage of your journey. Second, you leverage skills or knowledge that may be superior to yours so you can invest your time in leading the overall effort.

CASE IN POINT: SELECTING A SHERPA

An international industrial supply company decided to implement a new travel policy for all staff, which included guidelines for both physical and electronic data security. One of the salespeople shared that her sister was a cyber-security specialist, so this employee was asked to lead the implementation of the data security portion of the employer's change effort by educating colleagues on specific behaviors for keeping data secure.

Each sherpa is accountable for both guiding the rest of the team to the specific summit and transitioning to the next sherpa. Failing to include that accountability for transitioning to the next sherpa could result in delays to your change effort due to a lack of communication within your team.

Exercise: Selecting Your Sherpas

Jot down the first names of each member of your team, other than yourself, and the specific skills they possess that could support your change effort.

_____

_____

_____

_____

Now jot down the small summits you will reach on the way to your destination peak and the first name of the team member who could be your sherpa to that summit. Pick only one team member per summit.

_____

_____

_____

_____

COMMUNICATION AND HANDLING BACK-OUTS

The transition from planning to doing begins when you set an Up-Front Contract with your team for your change effort. An up-front contract is a Sandler technique that creates mutual agreement between you and all members of your team at the beginning of an interaction about what will happen during that interaction and its expected outcomes.

Your change up-front contract will cover the interaction's:

1. Purpose: The *why*, *why now*, *why that change*, and your destination peak.

2. Time: The deadline for reaching your destination peak with a *because.*

3. Your expectations: How you expect team members to support your change with specific, behavior adjustments and accountabilities and the consequences for non-support.

4. Their expectations: How team members can expect you to support them during your change effort.

5. Outcomes: The positive results of successful implementation for your team and the organization.

Remember, while you are talking about a change, what you are setting up with your up-front contract is a transition for each member of your team. Your outcomes must lead with the positive outcomes for them first.

CASE IN POINT: DELIVERING AN UP-FRONT CONTRACT TO YOUR TEAM

Sasha was the CEO of a business selling a software-as-service program used by human resource professionals. She believed that her company could grow more effectively if her service delivery team, which included implementation and customer care, began seeking opportunities to upsell and cross-sell existing clients and either close those opportunities or hand the opportunity to that client's account manager to discuss with their client. Sasha met with Brianne, director of service delivery, to discuss this change.

SASHA: Brianne, we've had discussions in the past about

the service delivery team becoming lead generating and even revenue generating. My belief is that, within 12 months, we could be growing 6–8% just through opportunities that your team identifies and, possibly, closes. If that continues, we could become the number two company in our space if not number one in three to four years. How's that sound to you?

BRIANNE: Sounds OK, Sasha. Not sure why you want to lay this on my team and me now.

SASHA: That's a fair question. We're getting pressure on two fronts. First, the current number two company is actively seeking an acquisition to leapfrog number one. Second, the board asked me at our meeting last month if I would be open to selling the company if an offer came through. I have no desire to sell, but our chair shared with me that some on the board don't see us continuing to grow. They believe an exit is best. My feeling is that if we can show that we can continue to grow, and we have a plan to overtake number two, the board will quiet the exit talk, and we can continue to build on the great company we have now. How do you feel about that?

BRIANNE: It's starting to make more sense. I don't know that I'd share the acquisition stuff with my team. That might panic a couple of them. What you're proposing isn't going to happen overnight. You've probably got a plan to get this started?

SASHA: Yes, I do. Before we get to that, are you comfortable talking about what happens when we are successful making your team a revenue-generating part of the company?

BRIANNE: Sure.

SASHA: If memory serves me correctly, you talked about wanting an expanded role in the company at your last performance review. Is that still the case?

BRIANNE: Yes. I feel like I've tapped out the development I can achieve by leading the service delivery team.

SASHA: You're going to be experiencing a lot of development over the next six months as you get your team comfortable identifying new opportunities with existing clients, and then getting them effective at closing new opportunities. If you're successful, I could see you expanding your role in the company.

BRIANNE: What do you have in mind?

SASHA: Currently the sales team reports to me. It might make sense to have the revenue-generating teams in the business report to one person.

BRIANNE: So I'd be the Director of Revenue?

SASHA: Let's not get ahead of ourselves. First, we must have your team members adapt their behavior, so they're proactively seeking opportunities with existing clients.

BRIANNE: OK. What's that look like?

SASHA: We're going to start small. For the next month beginning next Monday, the expectation would be that each team member would ask for 20 introductions from existing clients. That works out to about one per business day. We'll have training Monday morning to give team members some tools to make asking for introductions part of their regular conversations with clients, so they don't feel like they are going into "sales mode" when they ask. Are you OK with that?

BRIANNE: Yes, because you have the training already scheduled. That was my biggest concern, along with reassuring them that we aren't asking them to be quota-carrying salespeople.

SASHA: Correct. We're just asking them to adapt their behavior a little. At the end of each week, I'll expect a report from you with the number of introductions requested versus the number of introductions received. If at the end of the month, some team members haven't asked for 20 introductions, we'll look at a performance improvement plan for them. If they have no desire to adapt their behavior, we'll see if we can find them a role elsewhere in the company or support their transition out. Fair?

BRIANNE: I'd like to believe that everyone on my team will embrace this, but I guess we have to plan for resistance.

SASHA: What support would you like from me, Brianne?

BRIANNE: Tell me where we go after the first month and what you would do if we're not on track.

SASHA: Good questions. We'll expand the behavior adaptation. Your team members will learn how to make proactive calls to clients to ask questions about their existing service and identify other opportunities to work together. We'll have two half-days of training on asking questions conversationally, which will include some time to role-play, so your team is more comfortable. Does that work for you?

BRIANNE: Yes.

SASHA: Good. As for staying on track, you and I meet weekly anyway. If I see or hear anything in your report about the introduction behavior that raises a yellow or red flag, are you OK with me asking you a few questions and maybe doing some role-play?

BRIANNE: Yes. I like the idea of role-playing. Sometimes, I'm not sure how to have a conversation with a member of my team when he's not performing.

SASHA: Sounds good, Brianne. I'll send a meeting invite to you and your team for the training session on Monday. Would you give them a preview of what's going to happen next week before the end of Friday?

BRIANNE: Sure. I'll do it in our regular Thursday meeting.

You probably noticed that Sasha didn't just roll through her entire up-front contract before asking for Brianne's agreement. Also, Sasha didn't follow a script by checking off purpose, time, her expectations, team member expectations, and outcomes in order. Outcomes came near the beginning of her up-front contract (6–8% growth), and purpose came in the middle (the board asking about an exit).

To have a true up-front contract, you must complete the five elements (purpose, time, your expectations, their expectations, outcomes). But, by being conversational, you are more likely to create buy-in from your team members because you don't sound like you're dictating to them.

Exercise: Your Change Up-Front Contract

Write down what you would say to your team to kick off implementing your change.

_____

_____

_____

_____

For an up-front contract to exist there must be mutual agreement between all parties. You can't show up in front of your team members, dump your up-front contract on them, and then expect them to support your change. When you're done with your up-front contract, you must ask if your team members are OK with what you just said. As they roll out your change to their own teams, they will also develop an up-front contract with them about supporting it.

When communicating your up-front contract, keep in mind that you must touch each DISC style present on your team. Some teams may not have a particular DISC style, and that's OK in the context of communication.

For a quick review:

- D-styles care about the 30,000-foot and bottom-line views. Essentially, "Here's where we're going," and, "Here's what will happen when we get there."
- I-styles care about the excitement of something new and that they will get to interact with others during the change. Essentially, "We've got an exciting new program to implement, and we'll need your help to do it."

- S-styles care about their colleagues being supported during the change, and hope that their day-to-day will be disrupted as little as possible. Essentially, "We've created several methods for reaching out for support during this change and after," and, "While we will need to get accustomed to a new way of operating, we will start with small adjustments and build from there."
- C-styles care about having a clearly defined path to your destination peak with proper quality-control mechanisms. Essentially, "Let me walk you through our step-by-step plan to implement and manage this change successfully," and, "We have included checks and balances to ensure that we don't make errors in our plan."

Now is also a good time to give your team a chance to question or back out of supporting your change effort. It may sound odd to give team members a chance to back out, but wouldn't you rather know at the beginning that someone wasn't planning to be supportive than finding out partway through when it could be more damaging? Your team members will only feel comfortable saying they won't support you if you give them permission and protection. Use their act of defiance as an opportunity to explore their reasons. They are likely not alone in their feelings, and they may be the only ones on the team courageous enough to speak up.

As humans tend to be poor listeners, you'll want to have supporting documents ready when you launch your change effort. Our clients tend to use PowerPoint presentations, frequently asked questions (FAQ) documents, and, as technology makes communication easier, videos, podcasts, Wikis, and secure group chats to answer questions during and after implementation.

THIS CHAPTER IN 45 SECONDS

- You can't predict or control everything that will happen during your change.

- Even so, you must make time to create a roadmap to ensure some form of guidance as you implement your change.

- Your team members, especially Millennials, expect you to create your change roadmap collaboratively.

- A simple, visual technique for creating that roadmap is the change timeline.

- You must manage ambiguity to prevent it from becoming anxiety or, at worst, fear.

- To check how you are doing in managing ambiguity, anxiety, and fear, ask yourself if you are providing a safe COVE for your team.

    ◊ Is your communication clear?
    ◊ Have you been communicating openly?
    ◊ Are you vulnerable in your communication?
    ◊ Have your managed expectations?

- The transition from planning to doing starts with an up-front contract.

- Remember to communicate to all DISC styles on your team.

CHAPTER 8

Managing Change

Recall back to Chapter 1: Change is external, which makes it an intellectual process, while transitions are internal, which makes them emotional. With this in mind, the management of your new initiative first begins with an emotional topic: your values.

EASE OF MANAGING CHANGE RELATED TO PERSONAL VALUES

"Your values" in this context doesn't mean whatever is listed on your company website under "our values." It means your personal values.

Just as your team members don't work for you because they love your company but rather to advance their personal goals, they also don't commit to going through a transition because they love the idea of change. They commit to going through a transition because they aspire to live their values the same way you aspire to live yours.

Your personal values aren't just words like "integrity" or "honesty." Those are boring tropes that have been heard by employees over and over from leaders who didn't demonstrate those values in their behavior.

Adults learn by imitation and repetition. If you want your company to become a customer-focused organization, then demonstrate that your values align with this change. You might work a shift in your call center, go on sales calls as "the new person," or reach out to all types of customers, not just the ones who contribute the most to your bottom line every year.

Exercise: Your Values

What are your values?

_____

_____

_____

_____

Write down the specific behaviors you do that demonstrate those values.

_____

_____

_____

_____

How do your values relate to the change you're implementing?

_____

_____

_____

_____

Your change effort is likely to fail if team members see you acting in a way that is inconsistent with your values. Consistency creates trust, and during change little is consistent. You will not always get it right, but when you are inconsistent with your stated values be vulnerable and own it.

CASE IN POINT: LEADER INCONSISTENT

Leader Steve had a stated personal value that "we all pitch in to support the team." His company was moving to new offices at the end of the month, and an expectation had been set by the executive team that everyone would stay an extra 30 minutes on Fridays to pack the office for moving. The Friday following that announcement, Steve left early because of a family commitment that he neglected to tell his team. At the next Monday morning meeting, several of his team members were upset.

STEVE: Good morning. Who wants to kick us off?

BOB (irritated): I do. I speak for at least a few of us who aren't happy that you ducked out on Friday when the rest of us stayed to pack.

STEVE: Sorry, Bob. I had committed to take my daughter to her basketball game. I thought I let everyone know.

> BOB: We didn't know, Steve. You're always talking about how "we all pitch in," and you didn't do any pitching in on Friday.
>
> STEVE: You're right, Bob. I screwed up by not telling everyone. What's one of the other things I talk about a lot when it comes to work and personal life?
>
> BOB: Family first.
>
> STEVE: Absolutely. Bob, if you knew that I stayed late Thursday and came in on Saturday to pack up, what would you say?
>
> BOB: Um, I'd feel kind of dumb for calling you out.
>
> STEVE (smiling): That's OK, Bob. I gave all of you permission to call me out if you saw that I was playing "do as I say, not as I do." I forgot to tell the team that I had a family commitment on Friday, and that's my fault. Fortunately, I don't have any more Friday commitments between now and the move. How are you feeling, Bob?
>
> BOB: I appreciate you being up front with us, Steve.

By owning his mistake, Steve prevented a small ember of discontent growing into a raging fire, which would have distracted his team members from continuing their transitions. At the same time, he asserted his alignment with his core values by asking a hypothetical in the form of "if you knew...," which put pressure on Bob to reconsider and then to stop being upset.

PEOPLE

Especially during times of change, you must remember that the lead dog sets the pace. It's OK for you to be worried, concerned, anxious, or upset about success. It's even OK for you to share those feelings with your team as long as you end with a positive outlook. You don't want them to think, "Well, if the boss doesn't think we can do it, then there's probably no reason to keep going."

Exercise: How to Express Your Feelings

Let's pretend that your change effort isn't going as well as you planned. It's too fast or too slow, your team is unhappy, etc. How are you feeling and why?

_____

_____

_____

_____

How would you express these feelings to your team and end with an outlook of possibility?

_____

_____

_____

_____

Even though you have lived with your change effort for longer than your team members, you are still going through a transition as well. If you are unable to own your feelings and express them constructively, then your team members will feel uncomfortable expressing their feelings to you, which will disrupt and potentially scuttle your change effort.

A contributing factor to the emotions your team will feel during their transition is your pacing, which we addressed under the setting expectations section in the prior chapter. If your team feels uncomfortable talking to you, they will talk amongst themselves. This situation could cause some team members to fall back into the denial or resistance stages of their transition.

CASE IN POINT: PACE OF CHANGE CONCERNS

Julia was leading her team through implementation of a marketing automation program. In week three of her change plan, she got the sense that a couple of team members, Sonia and Darrell, weren't comfortable. She met with each of them privately to test her suspicions.

Meeting with Sonia

JULIA: Sonia, may I ask you a difficult question?

SONIA: OK. What?

JULIA: My sense is that you're not comfortable with the pace of implementing our marketing automation program. Is that fair?

SONIA: Well...yeah, I guess it is.

JULIA: I appreciate your telling me. What's causing you to be uncomfortable?

SONIA: I'm frustrated that we can't move faster. I see all of the awesome things that this system will do for us, but it feels like every time I ask about moving forward the answer is, "We'll get to that next week."

JULIA: Makes sense to me. Let's say you could design the implementation plan, what would you do?

SONIA: I'd let everyone work at their own pace.

JULIA: Which means?

SONIA: Which means that if I check off my implementation task list, I could move on to the next stage without being held back by the slower members of the team, like Darrell.

JULIA: OK. I'm curious: If you were able to work at your own pace and you finished your implementation, how does that help the team?

SONIA: What do you mean?

JULIA: Well, we're a team, not a group of individuals. I'm not against your plan, Sonia, but I don't see how it benefits the team.

SONIA: Oh. I hadn't thought of that. There's really only so far that I can go until I need the rest of the team to complete their tasks so I can move ahead.

JULIA: Fair enough. What if you became our expert on this system? What if you educated yourself on how the system would operate at full implementation, and then gave us a two-minute highlight of what you learned in our weekly implementation meeting? I feel it would keep the rest of the team excited and pushing towards getting the system fully implemented.

SONIA: That's a great idea, Julia. How would I do that?

JULIA: I'll connect you to our account manager who can set you up with that information. I will expect you to have something to share next Tuesday, OK?

SONIA: Totally works for me, Julia.

> JULIA: One more thing. I expect you to get your weekly implementation tasks done before you do any educating on the full system. If you aren't keeping up your accountabilities, the education tap gets turned off. Fair?
>
> SONIA: That's fair.
>
> JULIA: Great. I'll connect you to our representative this afternoon.

By getting to the truth, that Sonia couldn't move as fast as she wanted because she needed her colleagues, Julia leveraged Sonia's need for recognition by setting her up to be the team's expert on their new marketing automation system. She also got Sonia's agreement to the consequence that she would lose her opportunity to be the expert if she wasn't accountable for her implementation tasks.

CASE IN POINT: PACE OF CHANGE CONCERNS (CONTINUED)

Meeting with Darrell

JULIA: Thanks for coming in, Darrell. How's your day?

DARRELL: It's good, Julia. Thanks for asking. How can I help?

JULIA: Well, I have a question to ask you that makes me uncomfortable, but I have to ask. May I?

DARRELL: Um, OK.

JULIA: Darrell, my sense is that you're not comfortable with the pace of implementing our marketing automation program. Is that fair?

DARRELL: Why would you say that?

JULIA: You're really supporting the team by helping your colleagues with their implementation tasks, and you're staying accountable to what you agree to do each week. But, it feels like you leave your list to the absolute last minute and put a lot of pressure on yourself to get your tasks done in a really short time.

DARRELL: But I like helping the team.

JULIA: I'm glad you do, Darrell, but that wasn't my question. Are you uncomfortable with the pace of implementation? It's OK to say so.

DARRELL: I don't know why we have to go so fast, Julia. Everyone is stressed out, and I feel like we're not taking the time to make sure things are done right.

JULIA: I'm glad you told me, Darrell. Thank you. I don't understand a couple of things you said. First, when you say, "Everyone is stressed out," what do you mean?

DARRELL: I mean that there's this tension that I've been feeling for the last three weeks. We used to be pretty casual with each other, and now everyone seems tense, like their minds are occupied all the time.

JULIA: Makes sense. We started implementation three weeks ago, and everyone took on a lot of extra responsibility. The other thing I'm curious about is what you meant by "not taking the time to make sure things are done right."

DARRELL: When we do our Tuesday review meetings, everyone gives the chapter headings of what they're working on, but they don't get into the details. I'm afraid that if we don't spend time on the details, we may end up with more tension and stress in the office.

JULIA: Thank you for clarifying. Darrell, when I announced this change how many weeks was implementation going to be?

DARRELL: It sounded like a lot is all I remember.

JULIA: OK. It was six. We're 50% done with our implementation. How does that make you feel?

DARRELL: Not totally OK, but I'm glad you reminded me that implementation was only six weeks. It felt like it was going to last forever.

JULIA: I should have been more clear since then, Darrell. What kind of details are you hoping to get in our weekly meetings?

DARRELL: I guess I'd like to see a progress chart so all of us could see that we're 50% complete. Also, if everyone gave me an update like the one I email to the group on Monday afternoons that would be great.

JULIA: The progress chart is a great idea. We'll do that for our next meeting. Tell me, how much time do you spend writing those emails on Mondays?

DARRELL: Oh, not too long—30–45 minutes.

JULIA: Hm. Do you know how many of your colleagues read your entire email?

DARRELL: I expect all of them do; there are important details in there.

JULIA: That's fair, Darrell. But have you asked them if they want all that detail?

DARRELL: Well, no. I would want that kind of detail, so I expected they would, too.

JULIA: That's natural for us to do. But when we're communicating, it's about how our audience wants the information, not how we want it. Does that make sense?

DARRELL: But what do I do then?

JULIA: How comfortable would you be doing a chapter headings email with a note at the bottom inviting your colleagues who want more detail to talk to you or email you?

DARRELL: I like that. Thank you.

Unlike Sonia, Darrell's need is for team harmony and correctness. While Julia couldn't tell him that she would make the tension Darrell perceived go away immediately, she did help him look up from the immediate future to see that implementation was halfway over so he could discover on his own that team harmony would be restored shortly. Also, by helping Darrell understand that his colleagues might not appreciate his lengthy emails, she potentially increased his productivity for implementing her change.

Whether your change effort is purely internal or not, your clients are involved in it. Going back to the RACI model, your clients must at least be in the informed group if not the consulted group if they will be directly affected by your change.

CASE IN POINT: CHANGE IN COMMUNICATION TO CLIENTS BACKFIRES

A consulting company had a policy of sending out weekly updates to its clients to keep them informed of progress and to share critical information for the upcoming week's engagement. The weekly updates had come from the president's email until the president decided to have her administrator send out the updates on her behalf. However, she failed to ask him to send the updates from her account.

A few weeks after implementing the new update policy, the president spoke with one of the company's key clients about a piece of critical information contained in the previous week's email. The client said he hadn't seen that email. When he was told the president's administrator had sent it, the client told her, "Oh, I deleted those because I wasn't sure what they were."

After checking with several other key clients, the president corrected this. The updates came from her email address, which immediately resulted in more clients opening those messages and fewer conversations with the words, "I never saw that message."

PROVIDE FEEDBACK

Be aware that if you aren't providing regular feedback to your team members, they will create and share their own stories based on the limited information they have, rumors they hear, and their personal scripts. Once you flip to the managing side of the change effort, your most critical role is to provide feedback on progress and increase the number of strokes you give team members to reassure them as they transition.

Leaders have four types of strokes at their disposal: verbal, written (both electronic and physical), touch (such as an appropriate pat on the back), and time. The latter is the best stroke you can give because time is your most valuable resource. A time stroke could be extra coaching, role-play, or letting a team member leave early, which is a stroke because he gets more of his own time back.

A challenge for leaders is that they can't stroke the entire team—they have to stroke individuals. One team member may love being praised in a group setting, whereas another may be unwilling to have anything done in front of peers. Instead, that team member might appreciate a quiet word in private.

Because strokes are tailored to individuals, understanding your team members' DISC styles as well as their preferences for public recognition will prevent you from unintentionally giving someone a negative stroke.

Make a commitment to give strokes to the individuals on your team each day during your change effort. Verbal strokes are typically the easiest to integrate into your behavior. Track your team's attitude and behavior, and make note of any alterations after you give a stroke.

Giving daily strokes to individuals on your team may make you uncomfortable at first, but because team members have an increased need for recognition during the change, you'll have a more committed, more productive team if you do.

It's your responsibility as a leader to prepare people and give regular feedback. You must have a complete understanding of the dynamics of change, including how your team communicates and their scripting. Without this understanding, your change effort will hit a series of increasingly strong roadblocks. Your failure to be prepared to manage your team members' individual transitions will strengthen their denial and resistance.

Exercise: Knowledge Gaps

You've probably noted any knowledge gaps in preceding chapters. Collect those below in a "hot list" so you have one reference point from which to expand your knowledge. Take a minute and write down where you feel you have gaps in your knowledge of change dynamics that might hinder you going forward. You'll probably have at least two or three.

_____

_____

_____

_____

Looking at your list, which knowledge gap would provide the most benefit to your change effort if closed (e.g., confirming each team members' DISC style so you communicate effectively)?

_____

_____

_____

What makes closing that knowledge gap more beneficial to your change effort than the others on your list?

_____

_____

_____

_____

What specific action will you take in the next two weeks to start closing that knowledge gap?

_____

_____

_____

_____

A must for providing feedback is making progress visible. Humans are largely visual creatures so telling team members, "We're on track," or "We're behind," doesn't mean as much as if they can see that they aren't going to reach your mountaintop at the current pace.

Also important to success is celebrating the small victories. You have thrown your team into a game that they don't know how to play. Amateur leaders will say through their words or actions, "Just go win, and we'll celebrate." Professional leaders create momentum through small victories—single steps up their mountain that build into success led by their team. During your weekly progress meetings, find something to celebrate as a team—even if that victory is just every member of your team taking one step.

High performers usually have challenges with the "celebrate small victories" concept because they see doing one of anything as not enough. Change starts with being better than zero. Doing one of something is a victory, especially if that something makes you uncomfortable. You don't have to stay at one forever.

Whatever came before is your new baseline. If you celebrated taking one step up the mountain yesterday, tomorrow you'll celebrate if everyone takes two steps. This process will build until everyone reaches the top.

Another critical part of managing change is addressing problems when they are a 10% issue instead of a 90% issue. A 10% issue is potentially annoying, while a 90% issue could stop your change entirely. The only way you get to deal with 10% issues as a leader is if you've given your team permission, protection, and potency.

CASE IN POINT: ADDRESSING A 10% ISSUE

Chris's team was implementing a CRM, which Chris chose because of its mobile capabilities. His team was out of the office 75% of the time. Chris tasked Dale with testing the mobile capabilities before rolling out to the team.

DALE: Hey, Chris. Got four minutes for me?

CHRIS: Sure, Dale. What's going on?

DALE: The app for our CRM is driving me nuts.

CHRIS: Oh?

DALE: I understood that it would sync both ways automatically and update my phone's calendar and address book.

CHRIS: And?

DALE: It definitely doesn't sync automatically. I almost missed a meeting with a prospect last week because I entered the meeting on the web version, which didn't sync to my phone like I expected. I only noticed because I found the "sync now" option buried in a menu inside the app and my meeting popped up.

CHRIS: I see. Thanks for sharing, Dale. What have you done to resolve this issue?

DALE: I called our supplier and talked with the tech support. It seems like there's a setting on our phone that's blocking communication between the app and the web version.

CHRIS: OK, so it's fixed?

DALE: Not totally, I need to talk to our IT group to figure out how to make all of our systems talk to each other.

CHRIS: I appreciate you sharing this with me, Dale. It sounds like you saved your colleagues from a major headache once we do the full rollout.

DALE: You're welcome, Chris. I'm glad I can talk about this with you.

Without permission and protection, Dale likely would have never brought this issue to Chris, and without potency, he wouldn't have had the confidence to talk with the supplier's tech support or the internal IT group.

ADJUST BEHAVIOR TO STAY ON TARGET

As you climb toward each mountaintop, you will likely have to adjust your behaviors to stay with your change plan. Filter your adjustments through two lenses.

1. **Always move toward your mountaintop:** Adjusting behaviors must move your change effort towards your mountaintop, never backward, and as little side-to-side as possible. Keeping your team members motivated requires them to see upward progress. For example, two weeks into implementing a new benefits program is not the time to go back to your vendor and ask about additional coverages. Set your plan in place before implementing. Additional coverages may be part of improving your business, but during change the best strategy is to crawl, walk, run. Don't go back to crawling just because you found it easier than walking. Keep advancing.

2. **Ask if the adjustment advances the change effort:** If you make an adjustment, will it benefit your change effort? For example, does implementing an additional module to your new software program after two weeks of your plan make sense, or will it cause delays? There must be a clear benefit on which you and your entire team can agree. If not, you're pushing your team back into denial and resistance.

Winners make choices. What's more, they know that inaction is a choice. Be quick to adjust your behaviors if you can confirm with certainty that you aren't creating progress, but only after you've given your team time to produce results. For example, we suggest to our clients that they will know within the first three weeks of a salesperson coming on board if he will work out. If he isn't doing the behaviors (prospecting mostly) that you expect in his first two or three weeks, it is unlikely that he will have an "aha" moment at month six and become a great salesperson.

The complexity of your change will dictate how long you wait for progress before adjusting. A general rule of thumb is if you haven't seen progress within one business week from implementation, you may need to adjust your behaviors.

It is more important to be proactive than reactive. If you require your team members to enter all of their data in your new project management program by the end of the month, then ask them how they plan to do so efficiently and what roadblocks they see. Don't allow them to manage up by delegating their work to you. Help them see potential roadblocks before they become brick walls. Coach them to discover ways around those roadblocks before they happen.

THIS CHAPTER IN 45 SECONDS

- Ease of managing change relates directly to your personal values.
- If you behave in a way that is out of alignment with your stated values, be vulnerable and own that mistake to create greater rapport with your team.
- Even though you've lived with your change longer than your team, you will still go through a transition.
- Transitions are emotional, so you will feel emotions. These emotions are OK to share with your team as long as you share from an outlook of possibility.
- At least one member of your team will likely have a problem with your pace of change.
- You must increase the number of strokes you give each team member during the change to provide reassurance, which will smooth the transition.

- As a leader, you must address your knowledge gaps.
- Humans are visually oriented so make progress visible.
- Celebrate the small victories your team achieves to create momentum.
- You may need to adjust your behaviors along the path to your mountaintop. If so, ask yourself if that adjustment will benefit your change effort.
- It is more important to be proactive than reactive.

EPILOGUE

This Book in Two Minutes

T hank you for taking your first step on the journey toward successful change through managing the transitions of yourself and your team.

From Chapter 1, you learned how your outlook of limitation or possibility influences your beliefs, which create judgments, which prompt (in)actions, which create results, which reinforce your beliefs, thereby creating a stronger and stronger belief wheel that becomes nearly impossible to break. You also learned how to adjust your outlook and beliefs to create new judgments, actions, and results and make a new belief wheel. You learned about the four stages of transition (denial, anger, exploration, and acceptance) that everyone goes through during change and the behavioral clues that will indicate where team members are in their transitions.

In Chapter 2, you were exposed to the DISC model of communication and learned how each DISC style (Dominant, Influencer, Steady Relator, and Compliant) likes to give and receive information. You also learned how to adapt your communication style to your audience and how your DISC style will affect your new initiative.

From Chapter 3, you learned about the theory of transactional analysis and how people's Parent and Child ego states create scripts that cause them to react instead of respond to change. You also learned that people will play games to get their emotional needs met instead of addressing their discomfort during the transition.

In Chapter 4, you were exposed to the 20/60/20 rule of change, how the angels, agnostics, and atheists in your organization will affect your new initiative, and how to work with each group.

From Chapter 5, you learned that the success or failure of your new initiative rests with you, the leader, and how to handle the challenges you should expect whenever you launch a new initiative.

In Chapter 6, you were exposed to the eight common consequences of transformative change and how to avoid, mitigate, or eliminate each one so your new initiative stays on track.

From Chapter 7, you learned effective implementation of your new initiative starts with planning and giving your team a *because* for the change. You also learned about establishing a base camp and how to determine if it needs to move before you start implementing.

In Chapter 8, you were exposed to how to manage your new initiative and the transitions of yourself and your team members. Because you live with your new initiative longer, at the start you are further through your transition than they are. Supporting them through the initial stages of transition is critical for effectively managing your change.

This book is the result of many collaborative experiences with my clients. I invite you to continue the collaboration by helping make this content better. Please share your insights into change and transitions on social media with me through LinkedIn or Twitter (@sandlertraining).

Hamish Knox
Sandler Training
Calgary, Alberta, Canada

APPENDIX

Asking Good Questions

Throughout *Change the Sandler Way*, there were multiple references to asking good questions. This appendix is designed to support your asking good questions through David Sandler's Dummy Curve and reversing methods and Sakichi Toyoda's 5 Whys questioning method.

When asking questions, your goal is to learn the truth or new information that will get you closer to the truth. David Sandler said, "It often takes three or more questions to get to the truth." This became his Rule of Three Plus.

Something else to remember when you are asking questions is to avoid getting "happy ears." This happens when the human brain experiences cognitive bias, which causes people to hear only the information that supports their current beliefs.

When using any of the questioning methods described in this appendix, it is critical to keep your tone soft and nurturing and your body language relaxed to invite a response from the person.

The purpose of using these questioning strategies is to invite conversation. Before you use them with your team, be sure to practice until they become conversational. Otherwise, you may impede honest conversation.

DUMMY CURVE

I learned the difference between "stupid" and "ignorant" from my high school history teacher. To him, ignorant meant, "I don't know," while stupid meant, "I don't want to know." The essence of David Sandler's Dummy Curve technique is choosing to appear ignorant to uncover the truth.

Think of a time when you thought, "I know why that person did that," only to learn that you were completely wrong. When you have an "I know" moment, that's a great cue for you to ask a Dummy Curve question.

Examples of Dummy Curve Questions

- **I don't understand** (e.g., "I don't understand what's causing you to snap at your colleagues. Would you help me?")
- **I get the sense that... Is that fair?** (e.g., "I get the sense that our new vacation policy is causing some discomfort. Is that fair?")
  - ◊ **Note:** If the answer is "no," you can follow up with a gentle, "Hm. I wonder why I got that feeling," and let the pause linger until the person answers.
- **Help me** (e.g., "Help me understand this from your perspective.")

- **Tell me more about that** (e.g., after a direct report shares an opinion, say, "I appreciate you sharing that. Tell me more.")
- **Let me see if I have this straight** (e.g., "Let me see if I have this straight. You feel that entering all of your tasks into our new project management system is going to make you less productive. Did I get that right?")
- **I don't suppose** (e.g., "I don't suppose there's a different approach that we haven't considered." Wait until a member of your team starts talking.)
- **I'm curious** (e.g., "I'm curious how we'll make this implementation successful.")
- **I'm wondering** (e.g., "I'm wondering what we haven't explored as an option yet.")

Note on "If" and "Any"

In the wondering example, the word "what" is used on purpose. Another way of wording that example is, "I'm wondering if we've explored all of our options for implementation." Humans are conditioned to give an automatic, reflexive response when they hear "if" or "any," usually "yes" to an "if" question and "no" to an "any" question (e.g., "Anything else you'd like to discuss?"). Occasionally one of your team members won't automatically say "yes" or "no." Since the purpose of your question is to seek the truth or new information, learn to replace "if" and "any" with "what" (e.g., "What else should we discuss regarding implementation?").

When you ask a "what" question the answer still may be "nothing," but by using "what" you give your team members an invitation to continue your conversation.

REVERSING

Reversing is the skill of answering questions with questions in a way that prompts your conversation partner to share more information with you.

Answering questions with questions can sound harsh to your team members so you must soften your reverses. Softening a reverse can happen through your tonality or a softening statement.

Tonality

Softening via tonality is best done with one- or two-word reverses, such as:

- "Because?"
- "And?"
- "So?"
- "Then what?"
- "Which means...?"

You must practice softening your tonality, or those reverses will break rapport with your team member (e.g., picture a leader using "so?" in a sarcastic tone).

Softening Statements

A softening statement is a few words preceding your reverse that softens it by giving your team member a stroke. You can combine them with reverses for natural transitions. Examples of softening statements are:

- "I'd be happy to."
- "Great question."

- "Glad you asked me."
- "Thanks for asking."
- "A lot of people ask that."
- "I get that question a lot."
- "That sounds important."

All of Sandler's techniques are meant to be conversational. Be careful about using any of the questioning strategies in this appendix, including softening statements, too often during a conversation or you'll damage rapport with your team.

CASE IN POINT: TOO MUCH OF ONE SOFTENING STATEMENT

Early in my Sandler career, I prospected the president of a small telecommunications company. He invited me in to meet with him and his partner. Whenever his partner would ask a question, I would say, "Great question," then reverse. I used the phrase so much that even I started counting how many times I said it. Finally the president's partner said, "Have you never been asked something that's not a great question?" To which I responded, "Great question."

All of us laughed. I said, "Can we back up a bit?" We had a successful finish to our meeting—without any further use of the words "great question."

A Danger in Reversing

Some of the Dummy Curve examples end with a period instead of a question, as do some of the reversing examples. A quirk of the human brain is that sometimes people interpret a question where one hasn't been asked. For example, the "tell me more about that" Dummy Curve question could be reversed back with, "Happy to. What more would you like to know?" You might then think, "I should tell them," and you're right, except that the questioner might not care about 90% of what you say next.

When both parties know how to reverse, there's potential for a never-ending loop of answering questions with questions. To avoid this, be specific with your requests or questions. For example, "I'd like the agenda for our quarterly meeting sent to me by email by 6:00 p.m. tonight." Your team member could respond, "In the body or as an attachment?" This is a fair question if you haven't established how agendas are sent.

You can also answer a question then reverse if the answer is information you intend to share (e.g., "When do we need to have our forms submitted again?" "At the end of next week. I'm curious, what prompted you to ask?"). In this context, you would reverse if you have a sense that there's an underlying reason why your direct report asked the question instead of you simply forgetting to share that detail.

The following examples are reverses combined with softening statements. Note, the softening statement isn't specific to that reverse. When you practice, find combinations that sound conversational coming out of your mouth. You'll likely find a combination of these examples, and the one-word reverse examples earlier, fit your communication style.

- **You start** (e.g., "Jenny, it feels like something's bothering you related to our new organizational chart. Want to talk about it?" "Sure." "Great. You start.")
- **For a reason** (e.g., "I appreciate you sharing that you don't like the proposed compensation plan for next year, Juan.

You must feel that way for a reason.")

- **We might have a problem** (e.g., "Great question about carrying vacation days forward, Paul. We might have a problem. Would you like to talk about it?")

- **Page 3/Page 7** (e.g., "I'm glad you asked about our product development plans for Q4, Deidre, but you're on page seven and I'm on page three. Are you OK if we back up a bit and address your question a little later?")

- **Let's pretend** (e.g., "Good question, Stacey. Let's pretend that XYZ happened. What would you do then?")

Whatever combination or reverses you use, your ultimate goal is to uncover the truth or new information as it relates to your team's feelings about and support for your new initiative.

5 WHYS

The 5 Whys questioning method, developed by Japanese inventor Sakichi Toyoda, seeks to reach the root truth of a statement or problem by asking five consecutive *why*s. Each *why* moves a step closer to the truth.

You may want to use this method on yourself when you seek the *why* behind your new initiative.

For example:

"I need to launch a new product before the end of this year."

"Why?"

"Because I feel like we're losing customers."

"Why?"

"Because our revenue numbers are down this quarter."

"Why?"

"Because we haven't closed much new business."

"Why?"

"Because we don't have many opportunities in the pipeline."

"Why?"

"Because we've been servicing existing customers instead of prospecting for new business."

This process would make you realize that instead of putting a lot of time and money into creating and launching a new product, you should invest time in supporting your sales team to prospect more.

QUESTION STRATEGY SUMMARY

No matter which questioning strategy you plan to employ, you will fail to uncover the truth or new information if you don't practice that strategy until it sounds natural and conversational coming out of your mouth.

Even if the strategy you choose sounds great in your head, the first few times it comes out of your mouth it will sound odd. Find a partner to practice with or at the very least practice saying the examples shared in this appendix out loud to yourself so you can hear them.

Asking good questions begins with practice and ends when you uncover the truth behind your team's questions or statements about your new initiative.

Look for these other books
on shop.sandler.com:

Prospect the Sandler Way

Transforming Leaders the Sandler Way

Selling Professional Services the Sandler Way

Accountability the Sandler Way

Selling Technology the Sandler Way

LinkedIn the Sandler Way

Bootstrap Selling the Sandler Way

Customer Service the Sandler Way

Selling to Homeowners the Sandler Way

Succeed the Sandler Way

The Contrarian Salesperson

The Sales Coach's Playbook

Lead When You Dance

CONGRATULATIONS!

Change the Sandler Way

includes a complimentary seminar!

Take this opportunity to personally experience the non-traditional sales training and reinforcement coaching that has been recognized internationally for decades.

Companies in the Fortune 1000 as well as thousands of small- to medium-sized businesses choose Sandler for sales, leadership, management, and a wealth of other skill-building programs. Now, it's your turn, and it's free!

You'll learn the latest practical, tactical, feet-in-the-street sales methods directly from your neighborhood Sandler trainers! They're knowledgeable, friendly and informed about your local selling environment.

Here's how you redeem YOUR FREE SEMINAR invitation.

1. Go to www.Sandler.com and click on Find Training Location (top blue bar).
2. Select your location.
3. Review the list of all the Sandler trainers in your area.
4. Call your local Sandler trainer, mention *Change the Sandler Way* and reserve your place at the next seminar!